of

WALKING IN RAIN

OCTOBER 5, 2012 – DECEMBER 31, 2012

MATT LOVE

"I like men who have the weather in their blood."
Henry Miller

©2013 Rain
Nestucca Spit Press
South Beach, Oregon
www.nestuccaspitpress.com
An Independent Oregon Press Publishing Books About Oregon
Printed in Newport, Oregon by Pioneer Printing
Cover Etching by Frank Boyden
Book Design by Amira Shagaga

OTHER BOOKS BY MATT LOVE

Let it Pour:
An Unconventional Drinking Guide to the North and Central Oregon Coast
www.letitpour.net (2002)

Beaver State Trilogy

Grasping Wastrels Vs Beaches Forever Inc.:
Covering the Fights for the Soul of the Oregon Coast (2003)

The Far Out Story of Vortex 1 (2004)

Red Hot and Rollin':
A Retrospection of The Portland Trail Blazers' 1976-77 Championship Season (2007)

Citadel of the Spirit:
Oregon's Sesquicentennial Anthology (2009)

Gimme Refuge:
The Education of a Caretaker (2010)

The Teaching Maxims of Karl Love (2011)

The Newport Trilogy

Super Sunday in Newport:
Notes From My First Year in Town (2009)

Love & The Green Lady:
Meditations on the Yaquina Bay Bridge, Oregon's Crown Jewel of Socialism (2011)

Sometimes a Great Movie:
Paul Newman, Ken Kesey and the Filming of the Great Oregon Novel (2012)

Ladies and gentlemen, I dedicate this book to rain,
and as the song by Arrested Development goes:
I come here tonight to give thanks to the rain,
so brothers and sisters please put down your umbrellas,
you won't be needing those today.

I also dedicate this book
to former Oregon Governor Tom McCall (1967-1975).
Everyone who has ever spent any time in Oregon has benefitted
from the unprecedented and bipartisan conservation initiatives
achieved during the McCall era.
In effect, these initiatives led Oregon to become
one of the most desirable places to live in the country
within a single generation.
Even though it rains a lot.

In *Sometimes a Great Notion*,
Ken Kesey wrote my favorite line about rain:
"Give me a dark smeary shiny night full of rain.
That's when the fear starts. That's when you sell the juice."

I await rain. I need it to fall. I want the juice.

Without rain, I can't launch my new literary endeavor: a little book on rain written in real time with the modest ambition to become the greatest book on rain in the history of Oregon literature. Right now, that book is Ken Kesey's *Sometimes a Great Notion*, set on the Oregon Coast in November.

I know I will have to transmogrify as a writer to top Kesey. Rain is the means.

Why does *Sometimes a Great Notion* hold the title? Because this novel rains words in all the eclectic and unique ways rain falls on the Oregon Coast—from staccato to torrent to barely a pulse. The prose ingeniously and miraculously mimics rainfall.

Why? Because the word "rain" appears six times in the novel's first page and is used as a noun, verb and adjective.

Why? Because the word rain appears 500, possibly 1000 times in the novel and animates everything from Teddy the Bartender to rivers to the reader.

Why? Because Kesey integrates the Sermon on the Mount with rain's culpability.

Why? Because Kesey hews a landscape from the hues of rain, which is, of course, a physical and literary impossibility. Or it was until 1964 when *Sometimes a Great Notion* was published and despised by the New York critics who used umbrellas and thought Gene Kelly dancing in spurious rain was the apotheosis of synthesizing rain with art.

Why? Well, read this passage from *Sometimes a Great Notion*:

> The Halloween clouds had continued to roll off the sea all the rumbling night—a surly multitude, angry at being kept waiting so long, and full of moody determination to make up for time lost. Pouring out rain as they went, they had rolled over the beaches and town and into the farmlands and low hills, finally piling headlong up against the wall of the Coastal Range mountains with a soft, massive inertia. All night long. A few piled to the mountaintops and over into the Willamette Valley with their overloads of rain, but the majority, the great bulk of that multitude gathered and blown from the distant stretches of the sea, came rebounding heavily back into the other clouds. They exploded above the town like colliding lakes.

Where are you, surly multitude? Fall and make me grin. If you do, I'll give you a subtle bow before the first walk of the season.

I will try to write the greatest book on rain in the history of Oregon literature, yet it might go unpublished except for the fact that I'm a publisher and will publish it as I see fit. Rain made me do it. Some Portland critics who grew up in the corn of the Midwest will dismiss this book as "uneven." I feel sorry for their ignorance and hope they unveil it by using the term "uneven." They traveled all that way on the third incarnation of the Oregon Trail and still don't get it. Rain is uneven and that casts the spell. Rain has never fallen the same way twice and I liken its varied composition to snowflakes, fingerprints and lips. Rain virtually never falls straight to the ground on the Oregon Coast. This book will reflect those signature uneven properties. You want uniformity, write about the sun.

What a preposterous ambition, to write the greatest book on rain in the history of Oregon literature, considering what I wrote in a journal kept during my senior year at Oregon City High School:

> 2.22.82
> The rain is like a sedative, a black bag over me. The sun is alive and I want to do something with it. When I get older, there is little doubt where I would like to live. Any place but Oregon.

Some thirty years later, rain has recently emerged as the most dominant force in my life. It provides me a special acuity and energy I do not currently understand. I cannot stop thinking about rain, and as soon as it starts raining, I will start writing madly about rain.

Rain!

In pursuit of the title, I want to become the Werner Herzog on and of rain. Obsession trumps malaise in art and life every time. I want to become so obsessed with rain that I flirt with insanity and brandish a water pistol loaded with rainwater at anyone who dares stand in my way. I will break on through to the other side and rain is the only road with no disguised, diverging paths because if you want to know the truth, rain offers only one gray path—straight into it, with absolutely no direction.

See what rain has done to me; it has imparted grandiosity and inculcated ecstasy. In my cursory research of books about rain, I discovered authors have written the vast majority of them for children. I'm going to write a children's book on rain for adults.

For three minutes I perused the *Oregon Weather Book* and *The Climate of Oregon* and then slammed them shut forever. They reduce rain to strictly numbers and records. I want to expand rain into the realm of alchemy and the existential where no Oregon writer has boldly gone before.

Other writers unfamiliar with Oregon have written about rain. Other Oregon writers unfamiliar with the Oregon Coast have written about rain. But how can you truly write about rain unless you've experienced its quintessence? That would be here, where I live. I imagine there are rock critics who have never played music. I imagine there are food writers who do not cook. I imagine there are American government teachers who do not vote. I imagine there is a poet who has never walked through a clearcut who writes a poem about a clearcut. There might even be a Cardinal in the Papacy complicit in universal and conspiratorial child rape who believes he does good work for God.

Creedence Clearwater Revival poses the two ultimate questions of rain, ones I intend to answer: *Have you ever seen the rain? Who will stop it?*

I have other important questions of rain. Who are the rainy day women #12 & 35? Why didn't Bob Dylan use the word "rain" in that song? Why did The Beatles issue "Rain" as a B-side to "Paperback Writer" and not include perhaps their greatest song on *Revolver*?

The language of rain is primarily private but the practice of hearing it is universal. My hearing has made me want to write a book expressing its "liquid mystic theme."

November is three weeks away and I live on the Oregon Coast, a place where a direct hit of black latitude and white longitude (a small mountain range near the ocean) creates a perfect gray cloistering and geographical claustrophobia that produces an average of 300 cloudy days and 70 inches of "orographic" (the auto correct of my typewriter wanted to change it to "pornographic") rainfall a year. It is also a place that receives a vast majority of its precipitation in the winter, as opposed to other areas in North America east of the Rockies that receive most of their rainfall in the summer.

It can rain 100 inches in one year here. The record is 111. It once rained 6.1 inches in 24 hours. My record is experiencing 5.2 in one day. The word "pluvial" is a noun defined, "as a period marked by increased rainfall" and an adjective, "relating to or characterized by rainfall." The Oregon Coast is pluvial in winter.

That is the last time I will employ "pluvial" in this book. It sounds terrible, academic, dehydrated, castrated. I also loathe "dew point," a dull weatherman phrase if there ever was one.

Petrichor, however, is a glistening weatherman phrase if there ever was one. It is a righteous noun and defines the scent of rain on dry earth. Do you think any weatherman ever said "petrichor" during a broadcast? There had to be one visionary out there, somewhere, probably now unemployed, writing her novel in longhand in a dive Pacific Northwest bar as rain falls like cheap Pacific Northwest lager from a black sky.

This restlessness for rain has pushed me to the brink of insanity. Fall on me! I have grown so bored with sunshine that I have taken to rewriting the lyrics of songs about rain. For example, "Bus Stop" by the Hollies:

Bus stop, wet day, she's there, I say
Please kill your umbrella
Bus stop, bus goes, she stays, love grows
Under no umbrella

All that winter we enjoyed it
Wind and rain and shine
That umbrella, we destroyed it
By August, she was mine

I recently finished a biography of James Cain, author of *The Postman Always Rings Twice* and *Mildred Pierce* and came across a line that startled me. This is a paraphrase: "A writer with ambition has to become a pelagic fish," meaning he has to swim out to open water where it's deep, where he could drown and no one would ever know.

Is rain deep? Is there any chance a book on rain could end up a success? A lucrative deal where I sign a fat contract in a big city where people wield umbrellas as fashion and fly to private beaches and artificial lakes in corporate deserts to consider manuscripts?
What is success in writing? What is ambition? I don't know, but I do know I want to write about rain in a way no one ever has before. Perhaps I will include some science, but I much prefer impressionism to meteorology and making mix tapes to storing music in non-existent clouds. As John Steinbeck wrote in *The Log from the Sea of Cortez*, "Let's see what we see, record what we find, and not fool ourselves with conventional scientific strictures."

Sometimes, however, I prefer the strictures of science when investigating a story, especially when it unleashes abstract thinking that undermines conventional wisdom or writing about a subject—like rain.

How about this for a little science? My colleague across the hall, the Mormon math teacher, the best teacher I have ever worked with, answered a question I posed to him one rainy morning: what is the weight of all rain that has fallen on me since I moved to the Oregon Coast in 1997?

Upon hearing this, he became visibly excited at the prospect of solving a heretofore unasked question of math and the human condition. Rain does that to people. It makes you want to know. Thirty minutes later, he came up with the following solution and wrote it on the whiteboard with dizzying speed. I barely know what any of it means:

Average Rainfall for Oregon Coast = **70** *inches per year*

Time on Oregon Coast = **15** *years*

Total Rainfall in 15 Years = $70 \frac{in}{year} \times 15\ years = 1050\ inches\ of\ rain$

Waist Size of Author = **30** *inches*

Circumfrence of a Circle = $2 \cdot \pi \cdot r$ (*r is the radius*)

$$\text{Author's Waist as a Circle Yields an Average Waist Radius} = \frac{30\ inches}{2 \cdot \pi} \approx 4.8\ inches \Rightarrow 5\ inches$$

Author's Cross-Sectional Area = $\pi \cdot r^2 - \pi \cdot (5\ inches)^2 = 78.5\ in^2 \Rightarrow 80\ in^2$

Volume of Water Over 15 Years = $1050\ in \cdot 80\ in^2 = 84000\ in^3$

Density of Water = $0.036\ lbs/in^3$

Mass of Water on Author in 15 Years = $84000\ in^3 \cdot 0.036 \frac{lbs}{in^3} = 3024\ lbs \approx 3000\ lbs = 1.5\ tons$

One and a half tons. The weight of my rain.

Could such a book about rain on the Oregon Coast have application to other places it rains? Could readers in those other places, including the sad Umbrella Lands, extrapolate anything useful from my excursions and discursions in rain? Who knows? I have no idea what I'm going to write about, a blind lack of recognition entirely new to me when beginning a new book. I have only one objective—win the title.

My portable Italian typewriter, rescued from a thrift store, a virgin, stands ready to pound out this tome. I choose to write on a typewriter because the sound of a manual typewriter in action almost exactly replicates the sound of hard rain hitting the skylights of my cabin. Furthermore, I'm into tactile things these days and if rain is nothing else, it is tactile. Rain will never suffer digitization, although it can be used and disabused. Remember the 1980s and their concomitant hair metal bands? Remember all those overwrought videos of power ballads? They were the phoniest use of rain in the history of rain. Contrast the video of "November Rain" by Guns N' Roses with the films *Bladerunner, Apocalypse Now, Say Anything, The Shawshank Redemption* and *Seven Samurai*—schlock versus opera.

Unfortunately, a record dry spell persists and I grow bored sitting on my deck, shielding my eyes from the accursed sun, and daydreaming of rain and its sensuality. To pass away the hours, I keep listening to one of the greatest rain songs of all time: The Temptations' "I Wish it Would Rain."

> *Sunshine blue skies please go away*
> *The girl has found another and gone away.*
> *With her went my future my life is filled with gloom*
> *So day after day I stay locked up in my room.*
> *I know to you, it might sound strange but I wish it would rain.*

That pretty much summed up the winter of 2011-12 except that I didn't stay locked up in my room after she found another and disappeared. I ventured outside to explore rain and confront the serrated truth about myself while she traveled first class to where the sun always shines and foreign capital enslaves locals and monkeys to exploit the sun for profit and banal New Age insights.

During this confrontation, I was reading Jacques Cousteau's incredible memoir *The Silent World*, and marveling at his pioneering zeal to explore under the sea with his invented, finagled equipment. He wrote, "Sometimes we are lucky enough to know that our lives have been changed, to discard the old, embrace the new, and run headlong down an immutable course."

Actually, I marched down my immutable course and it was raining, raining, raining. In the aftermath of the breakup, I suffered an almost debilitating emotional crisis but decided to stand up and walk right into rain in hope of discovering a secret passage through the misery. I found it. I embraced rain and let it transfigure me.

I can't envision where this book really begins, let alone will end. I'll just follow E.L. Doctrow's lead, "Writing is an exploration. You start from nothing and learn as you go."

One thing I do know: this book will unfold like that scene from *Apocalypse Now* when Martin Sheen's Captain Willard steps on the boat to begin his secret mission upriver, and the pilot says, "I don't know where we're going, but one look at you and I know it's going to be hot."

Actually "wet." It will be a real choice mission.

OCTOBER 12, 2012

Last night, in bed with Sonny the old husky snoring by my side, I watched Ridley Scott's *Prometheus*, an inane science fiction film that posits human beings originated not from rain but aliens.

Three quarters of the way through the movie, I heard the clatter of one or two tiny reindeer on the roof. Must be scouts for the Big Rain Man, I thought. He was uncharacteristically late this fall and Oregonians were clamoring for his gift. It was all over the news and social media. Sure they clamor, but most of the weaklings and dilettantes recant the sentiment in two days. In two weeks, they've offered puny terms for surrender.

I turned off the DVD player and sprang from the bed. I threw open the sash and waited.

The sleigh landed. Lovely petrichor. The longest summer/fall drought in recorded Oregon history was over. I wanted to run outside and revel, but I was too tired from battling a wealthy couple who had stolen 4000 square feet of Oregon's publicly-owned beaches near my cabin for their new garish beachfront mansion. Furthermore, I was exhausted from haranguing a feckless, desiccated state employee who aided and abetted the couple's thievery with his bureaucratic response befitting a Soviet apparatchik. Undoubtedly, the mansion will conform to the 5-2-10-1-2-2 mould: 5000 square feet, two plutocrats, ten television sets, one tanning bed, and two Christmas trees for the two weeks out of the year the interlopers visit.

Yes, I wanted to run outside and dance naked in rain, but there will be plenty of time for that. Rain has finally arrived and I can now properly begin this book.

I listened for ten minutes, fell asleep and dreamt of a shaman in rain, but it wasn't me. She was wearing black rubber boots, a green dress and tiny limpet earrings. She also carried a kelp wand of some kind, or maybe it was a sparkler.

OCTOBER 13, 2012

Rain makes a major debut; rain is thick with temptation, thus, Rain Creatures finally materialize.

I load Sonny into the truck and we head to the beach on a Friday morning. No school for me, although I will visit my classroom later to complete the paperwork necessary to take my students on the first field trip in the history of American public education whose official destination is "Rain" and official purpose is "Rain" and unofficial chaperone is the "Legion of the Damp." I wonder what my principal will make of that. He's lived his entire life on the Oregon Coast, so I think he understands.

The students thought me mad when I pitched the idea, but if it meant missing class, well, why not? The great thing about this field trip is that it doesn't cost taxpayers a cent and there is no preconceived outcome. We just wait for rain, a rigid rain, then walk right into the downpour, and experiment with various forms of confrontation ranging from the psychic to the tactile.

There's that word again, confrontation. Is it too harsh? Perhaps engagement is what I'm after.

Sonny and I descend the slippery path to the beach. Eel grass and kelp are splayed and disarrayed at the wrack line, as if they had died by withering machine gun fire from a pillbox. If only the grass and kelp were developers and I could see the smoldering remains of custom Humvees shot up in the surf.

Cruising north in a strengthening rain, I discover the largest limpet I have yet unearthed. I turn it upward to the sky, let water delicately pool in the shell, and then drink rain funneled through the keyhole. If someone sees me imbibing like this, they might think I've totally lost my mind.

A woman appears on the beach. She's collecting treasures in rain and holding an umbrella on the verge of upward collapse. I take a photograph of her with the old film Canon and recall the time I broke up with a woman who pulled out an umbrella when it started to rain and we were walking on the Bayfront. I couldn't be seen with her; I couldn't let my students see me. I snatched the umbrella out of her hands and threw it into Yaquina Bay where the sea lions came along and pulverized it. I just left her standing there, sobbing in a downpour, and kept walking to a tavern that served only cheap beer and wine in a box, a tavern my now-former girlfriend hated because there were no mirrors in the bathroom for her to freshen herself up after coming in out of rain. She'd never read *Sometimes a Great Notion* either, so obviously it was never going to work out between us. I can thank rain for that.

I never want a woman to freshen up after coming out of rain. Rain has just freshened you.

Sonny and I leave the beach to run errands in Newport. I drive us over the bridge as rain right angles through the arches of green steel. Things are slicking up, skids here and there, puddles, wrecks. One of my antediluvian mix tapes plays on the stereo. Here comes "My Wave" by Soundgarden:

Don't come over here
and piss on my gate
Save it, just keep it
off my wave

I see a man wearing the official rain uniform of destitute people on the Oregon Coast: dark hooded sweatshirt, pajama bottoms, energy drink, cell phone. What is he talking about while walking in rain down the shoulder of Highway 101?

Now it's time for the Rolling Stones' "Get Off My Cloud":

I said, Hey! You! Get off of my cloud
Hey! You! Get off of my cloud
Hey! You! Get off of my cloud
Don't hang around 'cause two's a crowd
On my cloud baby

We pass a church housed in a former automotive shop and I see a man emerge and open an umbrella. I thought he loved God and all His creations. It occurs to me that three churches in the Newport area call a former automotive shop home. Did they take the lifts out? Or does the preacher arise above the congregation with the press of a greasy button? I'd like to see that spectacle.

I think I would like to start my own church, the Oregon Church of Rain, and become a minister of rain or the Frederick Douglass of rain, championing the emancipation of rain from the pulpit, while out in the pews segregationists mass under fancy golf umbrellas with corporate logos.

My church would worship rain, read rain as scripture, and taste sacramental rain from shot glasses. We would venerate no broken bodies and purge all the judgmental sands from the Mesopotamian deserts because the plasma in our bodies is basically seawater. We would take rain intravenously as a ritual but wouldn't require a needle. We would burn umbrellas at the stake and dance around the fire. We would anoint an angel of rain and her name would be Sky.

Sonny is the only member of the Oregon Church of Rain. She'll need a new paisley collar for that status, but not a bath.

OCTOBER 15, 2012

When anger comes, what do you do with rain? You advance into it and watch the various medical spiritual metaphors mix and play: tourniquet, poultice, compress, stitches, ablution, irrigation, baptism, anointing. Choose one and make it work or become dangerous or endangered.

Rain rips sideways through the neighborhood. Wind gusts of 50 miles an hour tend to do that.

I don the pea coat and stuff a digital camera into a pocket full of sand and limpets. Time to venture into the deluge and document the afore-mentioned obscene theft of sacred sand to protect a vainglorious invest-ment from its inevitable and justified burial at sea.

Did you know that Jesus was the first land use planner? "Build on a rock," he said. Not sand and a bulwark of transient riprap.

I photograph the ugliness in anger and then detour through the neigh-borhood to photograph beauty—the various mermaid statues posing in their various states of gorgeous decay, becoming smoother and smoother as decades of rain efface contours and perfections. Is that the ultimate manifestation of rain on the Oregon Coast—a smoothing effect? Has rain smoothed or roughened me out? Both at the same time?

OCTOBER 21, 2012

From where I stand in a rainy barrage on my deck, I can see the sun on my neighbor's dry tar roof. It's raining like the Battle of Stalingrad: moving block by block, house to house.

Normally, I would race to my local unnamed beach, the one I christen with a new name every week, and watch rain collide with the ocean, one of the more serene applications of nature and completely unavailable to download to any phone or computer.

But I can't go to the Hank Stamper Memorial Beach. The hideous riprap protecting the theft has enraged me and I absolutely loathe returning from my walks in such a vitriolic state. It makes the soul sick.

Thus, I will go somewhere else. I load Sonny into the truck and we go to meet rain at Ona Beach. Some unpredictable and soothing act of magic always occurs at Ona and I can never predict what source will generate it. Could be Russian Old Believers playing golf. Could be salmon riding a freshet up Beaver Creek. Could be a teal wave breaking in Emily Dickinson fashion—slant.

We hit the beach and see no other humans. About a hundred gulls sit in the estuary debating something.

The sky hovers like a jagged black and gray layer cake and showers blow lightly from south to north. Then there is light, but also more rain from the edges. Seconds later, a quarter of dim rainbow explodes from the cake and sinks into the ocean. I extract my cheap digital camera from the pocket of my corduroy coat and start shooting away. More light manifests and better illuminates the rainbow. The cake dissolves and out jumps a full rainbow. Then a double rainbow fades into view and reflections of rainbows appear everywhere on the sand. I walk on rainbows. Is this the true definition of psychedelic?

Sonny and I start running to the rainbow, which arcs so huge I can't capture it entirely in the frame. Yes, we run, in rain, because we know of the rainbow's elusive, ephemeral nature. At some point, when the light seems perfect, I halt, set the camera on self-timer, anchor it in the sand, and take more photographs.

The rainbow festival lasts 20 minutes and several cars pull off Highway 101 to witness the spectacle and wave at me. As Sonny and I leave the beach in rain, I feel invigorated documenting beauty as opposed to desecration. On the drive home listening to Led Zeppelin, the greatest rain band of all time, I formulate an interesting new existential axiom: in the long run, rainbows disintegrate the riprap of people's minds.

OCTOBER 23, 2012

Henry David Thoreau suggested that if "One advances confidently in the direction of his dreams…he will meet with success unexpected in common hours." He also wrote, "Again it rains, and I turn about. The air excites me. Yesterday all was tight as stricture on my breast; today all is loosened."

These days, I'm all about advancing to meet with unexpected success, so, out of sheer curiosity and novelty, I tried to dream of rain last night to loosen things up.

Nothing happened, although rain did fall in impotent showers, producing little drum rolls on the roof. In fact, rain, as it so often does, kept me awake, insisting I listen to its sounds, insisting I write this meandering little book.

The last Presidential debate occurred yesterday evening. I didn't watch it because I haven't watched television in 12 years. I have never heard the sound of Mitt Romney's voice, which is a good thing, I think. One wonders: which candidate, given the gratuitous opportunity in a Sun Belt state, would best inveigh rain? Both contenders are clearly sun people and vacation in expensive sunny places. "What do politicians do with rain?" I always ask students during our study of Oregon rain. I'll never forget one of the answers: "They use it to create fear," wrote a senior who used to walk to school in rain wearing pajamas.

The rain dream never materialized even though I conducted an elementary "directed dreaming" procedure before going to bed to induce rain into my subconscious, where to my knowledge, it has never surfaced. I followed the procedure exactly how I delineate it to my WR 121 students in preparation to write essays on dreams. I ask them to dream to discover something crucially unknown in their lives, and they all enthusiastically try the procedure. Why not? Twelve years of public education has provided few, if any, enlightening answers to many of their questions on the core issues of humanity. "Dream on," sang Aerosmith, and make it homework. I might even grade it, if such a thing was possible or desirable.

The procedure:

   A) Students should prepare their rooms and themselves for the dream initiation and recording ritual: have journal and pen by bedside; no music or television noise; light candles or incense for effect; turn off your phone; dim lights or proceed in total darkness.

   B) Get into restful state and then say the directed dreaming statement to yourself: "Tonight I want to dream and discover *(insert whatever it is they want to discover here)*. When I wake up, I will record three words or the entire dream in my journal."

As I said, rain didn't fall in my dreams, but I wanted to discover something else and I said that thing aloud too.

Nothing happened on that front either.

OCTOBER 28, 2012

March 30, 1840
From Henry David Thoreau's journal:

Pray what things interest me at present? A long, soaking rain, the drops trickling down the stubble while I lay drenched on last year's bed of wild oats.

This passage mesmerizes me and I copy it word for word in my journal:

Pray what things interest me at present? A long, soaking rain, the drops beating up the kelp while I lay drenched on this year's bed of virgin sand.

Some sentences on rain written today under the influence of primordial rain: I want to overthrow the hegemony of the sun. I drink the champagne of Oregon rain from a vermiculated black bottle. Speaking of vermiculated, most Oregon Coast pennies sport traces of green patina, usually at the edges of Lincoln's portrait. I want to be the Tom Petty, Henry Miller, Harriet Tubman, Steve Prefontaine, Hunter S. Thompson, John Lilly, Gale Sayers and Daniel of the lion's den of Oregon rain. I know the Milli Vanilli of Oregon rain—he's a charlatan of a writer—and I should call him out in rain. What would result is not unlike what happened to the Wicked Witch when Dorothy doused her with rainwater. Thoreau wanted to visit Oregon, but he never made it. I wonder what Charles Bukowski would have thought of our rain? He once wrote, "People run from rain but sit in bathtubs full of water," so I think he might have enjoyed it. Through my wanderings in rain, I found possibilities. In the sun, I found none. It is easy to be a saint in rain and avoid the darkness on the edge of town where it never rains. Rain is born to run, the sun born to sit in a soft chair. Was I born to rain? Rain sounds like Nirvana, the Pacific Northwest rock band; the sun sounds like elevator jazz. I want to write one riff about rain as memorable as the riff in "I Can't Get No Satisfaction." I typically get the blues whenever the sun shines brightly and never write much of consequence in the summer. No bluesman has ever written a song lamenting the appearance of the sun. I am writing that song in book form right now. Rain is wanton, exciting, the sun constant, boring. Rain gallivants, the sun merely beams. Rain inebriates, the sun makes you drowsy. Rain ruins guns, the sun keeps powder dry. Rain invites prestidigitation, the sun casts mere shadows. I never require gadgets in rain, especially digital ones; I reject all gadgets as potential keys to understanding rain's splendor or the universal equation of Esperanto. I have never owned a rain gauge and I never will. By the way, what is the equation for rain? I calculate it every day it rains, which means I'm doing a lot of unmathematical math. There is no map of rain; the sun is a cartographer's dream. Prometheus stole fire from the gods. Who stole rain? No one. Rain was an anonymous gift. The sun compels people to pay for gimcrack gifts and dangerous indoor tans. Rain pays you a good Gothic pallor. Rain plays chess and solitaire with you at the same time. The sun plays no games. Rain sets up spontaneous stages for unrehearsed performances. Rain never has to justify its appearance. Rain brings mountains down to the sea. The sun can't do that. Rain stimulates involuntarily while the sun willfully anesthetizes. Rain exudes perpetual ruth; the sun often shines ruthlessly. True, cataclysmic floods can result from an overabundance of rain, but floods are inevitable, necessary and reminders of human limitations and arrogance. Rain generally abates pestilence while the sun often abets it. Rain is the rank outsider, the sun a cozy lobbyist. My favorite hobby is to peruse rain. Rain is an essay, the sun a tome. Developers despise rain; they love the sun. After a rainstorm, all the colors are true, not RGB. Photoshop automatically color corrects my photographs of rain to look like rain falling in Silicon Valley. Alfred Stieglitz photographed rain better than anyone except for every photography student I have ever taught at Newport High School. One study suggested that children living in places with heavy rainfall are more likely develop autism. The study occurred in Oregon. Occasionally, rain encourages you to remain indoors and have sex, as opposed to the sun, which nags you into mowing the lawn. Who would you rather hang out with? Someone playing hooky from work because of the sun or rain? Rain is a bindle, the sun carry-on luggage. You can slide in rain. You can smear rain, but never touch the sun. Rain sluices gold. Rain foments serenity. Rain launches sedition against conformity. Rain sends roots deep; the sun desiccates. The sun speaks in monologues while rain always dialogues. Rain is aural and visual and has body; the sun can't possibly compete with that Triple Crown. Only genuine awakening results during encounters with rain. The sun? Mostly relaxation or trying to forget. All my great notions manifest in rain. All my mediocre ones emerge with the sun. We can thank capitalism for making the word "acid" an obscene adjective of rain. The Hindu religion has a rain god. Noah's 40 days and 40 nights is a richer story than Joshua's sun standing still. What are the semiotics of rain? Is it a symbol for transparency or solidity? Earlier, I switched on Save Me Jesus Radio and a crooner crooned a maudlin "thank you" to God for taking him out of rain. The implication was that Satan lurked there. God I hope so! If I find him, we'll get right down to it. The terrain of rain is unknown, probably unsteady. It can, however, be surveiled and reconnoitered. I wish I could paint rain. Rain lubricates the organic machine and pedals the water cycle. Rain apprehends and distributes. Rain kneads wounds. I read 1000 ancient Japanese haikus with 100 mentions of rain but none of them truly captured the essence of rain here on the Oregon Coast, which makes perfect sense because the haiku masters who wrote them had never experienced rain here. Rain transmits everything and sexless, umbrella-wielding people transmit nothing. D.H. Lawrence loved rain although I've never read an elegant line of his about rain. Robinson Jeffers was a real rain poet, William Stafford, Richard Hugo and John Haislip too. But they wrote about rain; I live it. Rust never sleeps at the Oregon Coast. Mold either. Rain is the ultimate in evolution and revolution. I will die by walking into the ocean and return to land one day in a form of precipitation. I hope to fall as sleet. How long would it take for me to return as rain if I had my remains cremated and spread upon the ocean? Rain is action; action is consolatory. Rain insists upon important psychic initiative; the sun delays it. Rain never gives you the *whatever*. Occasionally, rain makes requests of me. I never see them coming but I always comply. Many times these requests occur while I'm teaching and rain is raising such a racket outside that we suspend whatever we're doing in class and listen. Then we laugh. When this happens, I abruptly change the lesson to rain. I can always find a way in. Rain is like that in curricular and extra curricular ways that the sun can never match. Why do people vilipend rain? Even corporations need rain, especially agri-businesses. Threat of rain culls the weaklings. Rain strops those who walk into it. Football is always more memorably played in rain. In eighth grade, I nearly drowned on a football field by recovering a fourth-quarter fumble in a muddy endzone full of a half dozen opposing players flailing in two feet of water. Technically, I was waterboarded by my enemy in pursuit of paydirt. Tennis is also more memorably played in rain. In high school, I loved playing tennis in Oregon rain, and because the season unfolded in the perennially wet spring, we played most of our matches in some form of precipitation. I was a master of a slick court and could float a drop shot dead in a puddle or hit a slice forehand up the line that skidded so low to the ground it was unreturnable. In tennis, when the sun shines, the better player usually wins. When it rains, the more eccentric human being always does. Phone booths provide a beneficent purpose on the Oregon Coast; they shelter the homeless during big storms. I've witnessed this social service for myself. I even called one of the few operational phones during a deluge and a man answered. We talked rain for ten minutes and then he read the graffiti scratched into metal. A few lines were about rain. With rain, the word "divine" becomes an adjective, and better yet, a verb. I have divined many of life's most important intentions in rain. Using an umbrella is like turning off the light before sex. Rain does not abide coiffed hairdos. Indeed, it relishes destroying them. Rain is democratic, the sun a hierarchy. None of the cruel, paternal, monotheistic religions ever originated where it rains a lot. They sprung from men, deserts and heat. Rain is a woman. America is not a nation of rain and it is intestate, forlorn. What would happen to our country if we elected a President from the Oregon Coast who knew rain and loved it? Nixon and the Bushes. Kennedy, LBJ, Carter, Clinton and Obama. Sun men every one of them. See how we are? There has never been a rain man in the White House because they never run for office. The traveler found Ozymandias in a desert, not a conifer rain forest. Humans have renounced their sensual connection to the earth. Walking in rain is the strait of return. Rain is mystery, the sun obvious. Rain is sonic, the sun silent. It can rain cats and dogs but rain is dogs and the sun is cats. I love the smell of wet dogs in the morning—it smells like victory. Portland once had a professional football team and its mascot was rain. Portland has a famous singer named Storm. I really should meet her. Portland has a bad ass rocker named Michael Dean Damron who wrote a song called "I Love the Rain." Portland has a semi-notorious statue involving rain: an East Coast businessman clutches an umbrella in Pioneer Square. I often pay homeless men to spit in the businessman's face when tourists are taking photographs of the statue. Portland also has a famous poster called "Expose Yourself to Art," where a man who would later become Mayor, Bud Clark, wore nothing but boots, a hat and a raincoat and flashed a statue of a nude woman on the transit mall. Powell's Books has a literary award called the Puddly and the trophy is a pair of galoshes. I want an Oregon artist to design a deck of rain trading cards. Some misguided rocker in the Pacific Northwest started something called "Rain City Rock Camp for Girls" and came up with an umbrella with tuning pegs as a logo. The sun is indifferent, torpid, while rain pervades, incites. The sun glints; rain splinters. Rain meanders; the sun stays put. Rain is incipient; the sun is the end. Rain effaces; the sun blinds. Rain is a semi colon, the sun a period. Rain doesn't need an article to introduce itself in a sentence; the sun does. Reflections generated from rain are the most beautifully mirrored images in the world. You can't listen to the sun or moon. They are mere celestial factotums. Look at their precise orbits. Rain is never precise. I'd rather fall in love with a woman of rain, not the sun or moon, but of course, rain isn't for everyone as I have discovered. Rain portends nothing. It means everything. Rain suffuses and infuses; the sun dries and delaminates. Raiment is almost the perfect ancient and mellifluous noun of rain. What a sensation it is to have rain slung at you from a black cloud of a slingshot! I case the Promised Land when I walk in rain. The iPhone's default weather icon is a sun. I can't change it to rain. In *Butch Cassidy and the Sundance Kid*, when Paul Newman rides the bicycle with Katherine Ross, the soundtrack has B.J. Thomas singing "Raindrops Keep Falling on My Head," but rain never falls, which is something unfathomable and unforgivable. It could have been the best rain scene in cinematic history. In "Purple Rain" Prince sang:

Honey I know, I know, I know times are changing.
It's time we all reach out for something new,
That means you too.
You say you want a leader,
But you can't seem to make up your mind.
I think you better close it,
And let me guide you to the purple rain.

Where exactly is that? I, for one, want to know and my quest won't cost a cent. Rain in Oregon is always free. Going to the sun usually costs a lot of money.

Speaking of Prince, who invented the modern language of text messaging in his lyrics well before the advent of text messaging, in "Raspberry Beret," he sang:

The rain sounds so cool when it hits the barn roof
And the horses wonder who u are
Thunder drowns out what the lightning sees
U feel like a movie star

How strange it is, but I always feel like an unknown movie star when I am walking alone in rain and Prince understood exactly why.

OCTOBER 29, 2012

I arrive home exhausted after teaching with a swerving yet useful intensity. Rain shifts back and forth across the yard in delicate, unassuming layers, and invites me to walk into it, shed the sweat of the classroom, dissipate intensity, let go of everything and see for miles and miles and miles.

How strange it is to realize that Johnny Nash thought exactly the opposite:

> *I can see clearly now, the rain is gone,*
> *I can see all obstacles in my way*
> *Gone are the dark clouds that had me blind*
> *It's gonna be a bright, bright*
> *Sun-shiny day.*

The sun can enable the seeing, perhaps, but how can it remove obstacles? In my recent adult life, rain has washed every significant one away.

Sonny greets me at the door and then goes right back to sleep on her easy chair. This habit started a few weeks ago and has sharply undermined my morale. I must walk daily, twice-daily, thrice-daily, with this dog on the beach or I will go insane.

She refuses to go, which somewhat reminds me of recent girlfriends. They never wanted to rise early with me and walk in rain. I did offer.

I plead. I cajole. I entice. I make my multiple cartoon voices. This talkative 14-year old dog my ex-wife picked out as a runt puppy will not move. Our long partnership is coming to a languid end. We've rambled 10,000 times down Oregon beaches together, usually during some form of precipitation. I can't imagine her lasting through the long rainy season of 2012-13. After she dies, I wonder if I will know how to walk on the beach anymore. Rain will never be the same without her.

She stays on the chair and watches me leave. Her face registers distance and fatigue.

I run in rain until breathless and down to the beach. Piles of twisted kelp present a novel literary opportunity: untangle the tubes and write something ephemeral in the sand with decomposing fiber. Rain falls harder, like lashing whips. I uncoil a 20-foot snake of kelp and construct a green, yellow and brown punctuation mark that contemplates my life on the Oregon Coast without Sonny:

?

Rain hurriedly recedes to a rolling mist and I walk for miles and miles and return home to find Sonny asleep in the chair.

RAIN: a love story

HALLOWEEN

I can't remember a word we said to each other that rainy night, but I remember everything important because of rain.

Looking out a window, I saw Tricia's car turn into the driveway. I ran out of my house past two jack o' lanterns glowing on the front porch, climbed in her brown Pinto hatchback, and gave her a kiss. As she drove us to a Halloween party hosted by her older brother, we noticed costumed trick or treaters unaccompanied by parents, roaming the streets of Oregon City in a light rain.

It was 1981, my senior year. Tricia, a junior, had appeared out of nowhere the first day of school and mesmerized me with her graceful beauty, fame as a swimmer, and actual presence in journalism, my favorite class. A week after our initial meeting, *she* asked me out and we went on a picnic. A few weeks later, she had comfortably established herself as my first real girlfriend. My mom absolutely loved her positive influence on my pessimistic nature. Tricia knitted me sweaters, cooked special dinners and once surprised me with a gift of a stained-glass mirror she made herself. We saw each other almost every night and I always let her drive us around town because I hated driving and preferred watching her instead of traffic.

For the party, I wore a gray double-breasted suit, blue fedora and carried the toy Thompson machine gun I'd killed Nazis with as a kid. Tricia wore a silver-colored silk dress right out of *The Great Gatsby* she'd sewn herself. We picked out the fabric together and then I watched her make the dress in front of me.

In the car, we listened to classic rock on her AM-only radio and talked about what to expect at the party. I'd never met her brother and he was supposed to be sort of a wild redneck. There might be drugs at the party, Tricia informed me; there would definitely be alcohol.

We left behind Oregon City and headed toward Beavercreek. The Pinto rattled down narrow rural roads, past cow pastures, horse ranches and tree farms. Many miles later, when Tricia pulled the car off asphalt and onto crushed rock, rain began to fall harder and ricochet off the hood into the night. The defroster hardly worked on one of the worst American automotive models of all time, so Tricia rolled down the window half way and rain found its way to her shoulder, spotting the dress here and there. She never complained or bothered to wipe herself dry.

We followed an unlit curving road through a dense stand of Douglas fir and hemlock. Every now and then, branches swept the car's roof and sheathed everything in rain. After a half mile, we stopped in front of a white trailer with a dozen older vehicles parked in a lake of mud where a lawn should have been. I didn't see any jack o' lanterns.

Tricia knocked on the door and we walked into a cramped living room where everyone was at least five years older than us. All of them drank beer from plastic cups. A Ted Nugent or Aerosmith album played quietly on the turntable and cigarette smoke filled the air. No one wore a costume.

Tricia and I found seats on a plaid couch and I held the machine gun in my lap. Her brother came up and greeted us with two beers. Rainier, I think.

Thirty minutes later we left the party without finishing our beers or saying a word to anyone else. It was only 9 p.m. and we didn't know what to do. Back in the Pinto, Tricia pitched an idea. She suggested we drive to her house, hang out and watch television. This somewhat surprised me because I knew her mom and stepfather were out of town and I wasn't allowed over if adults weren't present. But I didn't object and she was driving.

Tricia lived several miles from her brother in a large home of stone and logs set back in the woods off a long driveway. There was a canyon behind her house and firewood stacked everywhere. Her stepfather built homes for a living and trapped foxes and beavers as a hobby.

Rain let up as we exited the Pinto. We ran toward her house holding hands, past some flickering pumpkins lining the walkway. I left the machine gun in the car. Tricia pushed through the ten-foot high front doors, led me past a dozen species of small and large mammal heads mounted on the wall, and into a den where she turned on the heat and television and opened the sliding glass door that led out to a deck. She always wanted to hear rain. In short order, we started kissing, our shoes came off, and we went down to the yellow shag carpet. I shoved aside a cassette recorder that Tricia and I had used a few days earlier for an interview assignment for journalism. The tape was still in the recorder. She looked at me look at the machine and then wordlessly twisted herself around my body and pushed the red "record" button.

I reclined on my back and she sat on my stomach. I felt her thighs and started hiking up the dress. Drops of rain rested on her bare shoulders. I don't think we said a word to one another.

She stood up and peeled off the dress and let it float to the floor. There was no bra but still a little rain. She let me look at her champion swimmer's body for a few seconds and then slid her panties off. Then, without standing up, I got undressed. Tricia climbed on top of me and I remember seeing the head of an elk on the wall behind her. This was all new to me, a series of sensual firsts and fascinations that, really, have never been topped in the subsequent 30 years.

Tricia drove me home in rain around midnight and we didn't see a single trick or treater although there were plenty of smashed pumpkins creaming the slick streets. She idled the Pinto in front of my house. We talked about seeing each other that afternoon, a movie perhaps, or something in rain, which was always her preference. I kissed her goodnight and sprinted across the soggy lawn to my front porch. The jack o' lanterns still flickered with their mildewed grins. Rain had not yet extinguished them after a long wet battle.

I went to bed knowing I was no longer a virgin. I still have the tape.

NOVEMBER 2, 2012

Last night, the rain shaman appeared in my dreams again, but she wore a new outfit: a flowing red dress and green rubber boots decorated with sunflowers. Most incongruous, yet also alluring. We were in the Barge Inn, an ancient tavern on Newport's Bayfront. The elderly customers moved like melting glaciers—slow, silent, dignified. We sat at a window table and drank thin coffee to ward off the slumber of the leaden afternoon. Outside, rain poured from the clouds and streamed down an alley at a 45-degree angle to the window. From time to time, the shaman and I halted our conversation to watch the fantastic run-off.

I vaguely recall her name…Robin. She was telling me the most extraordinary story of how she first encountered coastal rain. She had hooked up a watershed restoration job online and driven to Oregon from the East Coast. She knew nothing of Oregon except its legendary pummeling rain:

> I pulled into the house with the woman I was staying with, and her whole front yard was just moss. I mean it wasn't grass, it was moss. It was raining too, raining gray if you can believe that, and there were huge sword ferns and a gigantic rhododendron, and I was like, "This is awesome!" I saw a slug bigger than my thumb and was just blown away. I got rid of my um-

brella in record time because I read somewhere that nobody in Oregon actually uses umbrellas. If you do, they just turn inside out, like in the cartoons. This place, I love it. It's all about the water, being born a Pisces like me, absorbing the rain.

Absorbing? I had never heard anyone use that verb with rain. I love verbs.

She interrupted her story and said, "What sign are you Matt?"

I had no idea she knew my name. "Pisces."

Our birthdays were days apart.

She looked at me and didn't say anything for a moment. At the bar, one of the glaciers moved half a millimeter and ordered a pickled grotesquerie, one of the yellow eggs.

"You get it, right?" she said.

"Get what?" I had no idea what she was talking about.

"Rain...the ocean, being a Pisces, being drawn here. It's pretty obvious."

I had never considered it in all my 15 years of living on the Oregon Coast.

"Aren't you a scientist?"

"Yes, but I believe it all the same."

And then she was gone

Rain has occupied seven consecutive days. The rainiest month on the Oregon Coast has lived up to its philanthropic reputation. Let the ungrateful weaklings complain.

I'll complain about something else: a disease is haunting Oregon—the disease of a cultural infantilism. All the powers of old Oregon's intellect and reason have entered into a holy alliance to defeat this disease. They have all utterly failed.

The disease is exhibited by adults in connection to the fortunes of the University of Oregon's and Oregon State University's football programs. And infantilism it is, naked, bawling, obnoxious, crushingly boring to witness. I would ignore its irritating presence if I could but cannot since it constantly invades my cultural space. Can Oregonians talk about something else, like rain, or their sex lives, or the death of rock?

It all brings to mind something I read written by the Italian author/intellectual Umberto Eco, "Sports debate is the easiest substitute for political debate." He wrote that before the onset of ESPN and the Internet. Let me also loosely paraphrase something else Eco wrote about big time spectator sports: those who watch and obsess over spectator sports are not playing sports. They have lost the ability to play.

UO and OSU football used to entertain me with their futility and Nike-less innocence. I pine for those halcyon days...such as November 19, 1983, when the most fascinating game of college football ever played took place in Eugene, Oregon. It made football history because of rain.

A fierce storm blew a driving rain across the field every second of the game, now known as the Toilet Bowl. Rain provided the offense, defense and coaching staffs for both teams. I remember listening to the game on the radio and hearing the announcers use a form of the word "rain" 10,000 times during the broadcast. That too, was a record. According to a newspaper account, here's what happened:

> Both Sides Retreat in the Civil War
>
> It had everything 33,176 football fans wanted in an Oregon-Oregon State game—except points. In one of the most bizarre games in the 87-year old rivalry, the Ducks and Beavers bumbled their way to a 0-0 season-ending Pacific 10 Conference tie Saturday afternoon in Autzen Stadium.
>
> Announcement of the final score probably had them rolling in the aisles at press boxes along the West Coast but the humor would have been lost on lovers of fine-tuned offense.
>
> Two hours and 46 minutes of slapstick comedy produced the sixth scoreless tie between the two teams and the first since 1931.
>
> The game film single-handedly could bring back Fractured Flickers to television. Oregon and Oregon State fumbled 11 times, lost six fumbles, threw five interceptions, missed four field goals and were penalized 13 times.

Rain made the teams gloriously inept and made sports history that afternoon. The outcome marked the last time a college game ended scoreless. This distinction will remain as long as Americans play football because overtime and sudden death scoring that began in the mid 1980s and ended any possibility of a tie, which I find sort of sad. Finishing in a tie is often a good lesson in life.

I recall the Toilet Bowl's ineptitude with glee as I run errands around Newport today with Sonny in the back of the truck. Earlier, this morning, we got soaked on our beach walk, otherwise known as a play date.

The radio begins "It Never Rains in Southern California," one of the most loathsome songs about rain, so I fish out a CD at random from behind the seat and extract Mudhoney's greatest hits. After listening for ten minutes, I conclude they frequently sound like an unrelenting rain storm, which isn't surprising since the band hails from the Pacific Northwest.

Track three, "I Have to Laugh," comes on: *Listening to the rain, I had to laugh.*

Yes. At myself.

Neil Sedaka claims he heard "Laughter in the Rain" but only because he forgot to bring an umbrella along.

I have never heard laugher in rain, although I have heard its many other mixed, nuanced messages. Rain sends them repeatedly while the sun communicates only one message, unmixed and blatant.

Another errand. I visit the Sandbar and see Amanda the bartender out front picking up cigarette butts and admiring the weight of rain on the purple and yellow mums.

"The drops are so heavy," she says while touching them. I watch beads trickle into her cleavage and think: *rain has a glistening weight, the sun, a dull weightlessness.* I might be in love.

I ask Amanda if she has a rain story. She ponders for a moment. "I'll think of one."

I keep moving. At the animal shelter thrift store, I score a Roseanne Cash cassette tape, *Seven Year Ache*, for a quarter. Back in the truck, track one, "Rainin,'" plays: *It's raining, raining in my soul...I'll do anything you want me to if you just get me out of the rain.*

Cash thought *raining in her soul* was a bad thing? Perhaps in Nashville, Tennessee but certainly not in Nashville, Oregon. You want to find true love in Oregon? March a prospective candidate into rain and wait for a reaction.

Back in the truck, rain batters the canopy and Sonny howls her rain song that I can't imagine living without. I turn on the radio, a little FM classic rock beamed in by a media conglomerate broadcasting in algorithms from Los Angeles. Their DJs sound like stoners in the sun. I want a local FM radio station with DJs who sound like stoners in rain.

"Touch Me" by the Doors plays: *Now, I'm gonna love you / Till the heavens stop the rain*

Wrong Jim, but then I forgive your pathetic ignorance of the romantic potential of rain, because, well, you are dead, grew up in Los Angeles, and wrote a great rain song called "Riders on the Storm." I'll also forgive you for writing "Waiting on the Sun" because you clearly didn't grasp that love dies slowly when rain ends. Moreover, Jim, rain waits for absolutely no one.

Three rain songs in one hour. This was no mix tape. They came from somewhere.

Something is happening to me. Or I should say, with me.

NOVEMBER 6, 2012

Election night in the Republic, or National Entertainment State, as Gore Vidal once called it. Vidal also said, "Proof of the failure of the American public education system is that Ronald Reagan was elected twice by landslides."

A while back I read a line by Robert Adams from a book called *Why People Photograph:* "Most people alive in the United States today have never had, for a variety of reasons, the full attention of a first-rate teacher, and our democracy is failing partly as a result."

Gore Vidal wrote about our failing democracy all the time, but did he ever write about rain? He didn't really seem like a rain kind of guy. I thought the same about Christopher Hitchens after recently reading his memoir and a collection of essays. It almost goes without saying that Fox News personalities and pundits like Ann Coulter and George Will have never contemplated rain. They have no language for it.

The two-party system is the party of neon umbrellas emblazoned with logos of pharmaceutical giants.

Where is the political party of rain? Imagine one. Imagine our lithe and soulful candidate for President. You know she can dance. Imagine our energetic yet sublime television ads. They'd all resemble Buster Keaton films.

I find it utterly delightful that historic rain back East affected the political fortunes of certain candidates. It perhaps even turned some voters into rain people. Where will their new political identity convey them?

The returns are coming in. No rain tonight. No story.

NOVEMBER 9, 2012

Friday Night. Rain at dusk, a gray collusion worth recording in my imagination. I sit in Sonny's chair under the skylights, listen, and take notes without writing anything down. She's on the couch dreaming of something grandiose.

Tomorrow I will drive to McMinnville and deliver a presentation to an environmental education organization at their annual fundraiser. My topic: "Landscapes in Ken Kesey's *Sometimes a Great Notion*," which means I will discuss rain with 200 people drinking fine Willamette Valley wine. I'll also read some of my favorite passages on rain from Kesey's masterpiece while I display black and white photographs taken by my students. I have never given this presentation before and have no idea of its potential trajectory. I will use no notes and the talk will likely unfold like rain. Let us all pray that the wine holds out. Rain always goes better with wine.

This sort of presentation isn't novel. Over the decades, other writers, journalists and scholars have mined rain for insights into the character of those who live, work and politick in the Pacific Northwest. They all have asked the same question: what does rain do to these people? They typically ask in the third person inside offices and cubicles. I am asking in the first person while walking in rain.

For example, I just finished an essay titled, "Rainfall and History: Perspectives on the Pacific Northwest," by Richard Maxwell Brown. It was the lead essay of an anthology called *Experiences in a Promised Land: Essays in Pacific Northwest History*, edited by G. Thomas Edwards and Carlos A. Schwantes.

"I shall focus on the way in which northwesterners have reacted to the pervasive rainfall in terms of ideas images, attitudes and emotions," writes Brown, a professor of history at University of Oregon when the anthology was published in 1986. His essay contains 58 footnotes in 12 pages. His thorough documentation assures us he knows rain.

Does he?

Brown gives the greatest book on rain in the history of Oregon literature one paragraph…"Ken Kesey depicts the dispiriting effect of the steady rain on the Oregon Coast…."

Dispiriting is the wrong, shortsighted adjective and Kesey does a lot more than depict. He imbues rain with an unruly consciousness. In the novel, rain commands a presence and disdains sublimity. By falling in ubiquity the way it does on the Oregon Coast, rain intersects with everything and influences all. Kesey's portrayal of rain enlivens or enervates people, frequently at the same time. Rain is a character, motif, narrative, sheen and a cocoon. Kesey nailed rain on a page like no other writer in history.

Brown culls the various documents and literature pertaining to rain in the region and offers a thesis: "And if calm moderation has indeed been the most distinguishing characteristic of Pacific Northwest history and life, is it not much due to what I have emphasized?: the supreme regularity of the calming moderating ambience of the Northwest's rainfall."

An alluring thesis, I will grant that, but one exclusively derived from an I-5, Seattle to Eugene outlook, citified, collegiate. No field work involved. No walking in rain where all the mystic knowledge accrues.

We receive twice the amount of rainfall Professor Brown describes as moderating. Never in a million years would I portray rain on the Oregon Coast as having a calming, moderating influence. In fact, I would say precisely the opposite is true and Kesey wrote the same in over 600 pages.

Brown is an academic and treated rain in academic fashion, which is proper, his right, and also entirely devoid of passion or engagement. Brown wrote a detached historical essay about rain. I assess rain with my eyes, ears, nose, mouth, hands and feet. I am mad to be in contact with it and pressgang everyone around me to feel the same, or at least give a try. Rain urges and urges me on. Not once have I ever contracted the blues because of rain, although I do love the Lightnin' Hopkins song "Blues in the Rain," and the line, *when it's raining, that's a time a man has the blues.*

In his novel, Kesey stood his characters in rain forever and turned them loose. Some of them heard rain as a "soft delicious, wet kissing." Another "disappeared in a frenzy of drink and despair to masturbate himself to death." Others survived by listening to honky tonk music.

I walk right into it and the harder it falls the harder I come.

As Kesey wrote in *Sometimes a Great Notion...*"you have to go through a winter to understand."

Not a winter in Seattle, Portland or Eugene. Here. What about 15 winters on the Oregon Coast? Does that make me a sage of rain? I like to think so. But as John Gardner once opined about writing fiction: "there are no rules."

There are no rules of rain either…except that…one.

RAIN: a love story

THE VORTEX

I expected to make Oregon literary history that day in 2004. A couple thousand people would throng to McIver Park just outside of Estacada and commemorate Vortex I, the only state-sponsored rock festival in American history. And they would gather there only because my lifelong dream of becoming an Oregon writer of merit had recently come true after so many years of procrastination and immaturity.

Vortex I unfolded in all its Oregon counterculture glory the last weekend of August 1970. It was a story practically undocumented and lost to history forever until it seized hold of me and revolutionized my life. The journey took four years of travel, research, writing and cost me $40,000, but in June of 2004 my self-published book, *The Far Out Story of Vortex I*, came out. One reviewer called it a "hash brownie" of a book, which was interesting yet fitting praise indeed.

During the summer of 2004 I'd relentlessly driven all over the state to promote the book, delivering 30 presentations in 60 days, some to very large crowds, others to three people. The tour would culminate at Mc-Iver Park where I would give a presentation on the festival, sell out my entire press run, and make $20,000. No other Oregon writer had ever conceived of pulling off something so daring. State park officials had built me a stage and given me free use of a group campsite. Forty of us intended to camp out and ride the magic carpet back in time. My friend Tom's rock band would play on the very field where the rock bands once played. My girlfriend Rose would skinny dip in the Clackamas River and dance with me on the very field where 100,000 people once danced. The press would proclaim me as a unique literary entrepreneur in true Tom McCall maverick fashion.

My triumph was set for August 22, traditionally the hottest day of Oregon's summer. The evening before, the heavens opened up all across Western Oregon and began to rain and rain and rain.

Rose and I had listened to rain that night and she assured me it would stop in the morning and the show would proceed. How could it not? It rained once a century on August 22 in Western Oregon and then only a trace of precipitation.

In the morning, standing in rain outside her house, I took a call from a state park official. She asked me what I thought we should do. It was still raining and expected to rain harder in the afternoon. Should we cancel the event? It was my call.

Rose urged me not to postpone. I had never met anyone who believed in rain like she did. She argued the event would be all the more authentic if rain didn't stop. She thought all the nudity in rain might be fun, like Woodstock.

I stared at the sky, imagined a muddy mess, and cancelled the event. My first thought was to go, as fast as possible, to Nestucca Spit, the beach near the Nestucca Bay Wildlife Refuge where I lived and served as caretaker. I asked Rose to go with me, which surprised me because I typically recover from disappointments at the beach in solitude and never bring along a phone. She said she'd love to join me. I drove us to Pacific City in a rain crashing so hard the windshield wipers proved utterly useless. I couldn't see much of Highway 101 and navigated from memory.

Rose and I barely spoke during the drive and I replayed my decision to cancel. I parked the truck and we walked out to the beach, a half mile down Spit until we settled in the dunes. No one else was around, which made perfect sense since a monsoon was in session. I couldn't talk.

We sat there for five minutes and then rain stopped as if a deity had turned off a spigot. Instantly, a course of action became lucid to me. I stripped off my clothes and sprinted 75 yards toward the ocean. I plunged in, went completely underwater, swam a few strokes, felt the rush of cold, tasted salt, looked west, saw a harbor seal watching me, let my feet find the sand, stood up, turned around, and saw Rose waving to me from the dunes.

I began running toward her and then stopped. At that precise moment, I remembered seeing Stevie Ray Vaughn perform at a Salem amphitheater in the summer of 1990. There he was, on stage, outside, ripping through "Couldn't Stand the Weather," when a rain squall materialized out of nowhere and sent down an Oregon flood.

Stevie didn't stop playing. He didn't seek cover. He got louder. The sky was crying rain and he found new and exotic destinations on the fret-board, drop by drop. It was the greatest rain performance in the history of rock and naturally it occurred in Oregon.

He died in a helicopter crash two months later.

I had completely forgotten about this concert until I stood naked on the beach. Right then and there, I channeled Stevie's stiletto rain and was reborn and reeducated. I had allowed rain to ruin my parade and by doing so, embraced pathetic cliché, and suffered defeat. The first and only rule of Oregon rain is: always advance, never retreat. Engage rain on all fronts. Become General Grant, never General McClellan. McClellan was timid, a dandy, a loser. Grant drank whiskey by the barrels and stood out in rain when giving orders to his troops. Advancing into rain is becoming General Grant, winning. All the compelling Oregon stories happen when you advance into rain. Nothing happens if you stay inside.

Later, I discovered three inches of rain fell in Estacada during that 24-hour time period, shattering the previous record much like Bob Beamon did to the long jump record in 1968 at the Mexico City Summer Olympics.

Had I advanced I would have set a record too. I will never make that mistake with rain again.

NOVEMBER 17, 2012

A minx of a rain is falling this Saturday morning and calling me out for a romp. Somewhere else in Oregon, someone is weeping and vulnerable because of rain. This frail person, mostly likely in their third or fourth year in residence, is seriously contemplating leaving Oregon because they believe it rains all the time. They can't take it anymore.

Leave.

I'm drinking black coffee and thumbing the pages of an old out-of-print book with possibly the best title in all of Oregon literature — *Oregon: Wet High and Dry*.

I read it some 30 years ago as an assigned text for an Oregon geography course I took as a sophomore at Portland State University. One of Oregon: *Wet High and Dry*'s co-authors, John O. Dart, was my instructor. For decades he taught geography at PSU and probably knew the state's climate and topography better than anyone alive.

Professor Dart was my first man of rain and I will never forget a crystalline moment in his class. He smiled somewhat mischievously when he said it. He probably reveled in debunking a received national myth about Oregon in front of a packed lecture hall full of mostly Oregonians. I imagine he felt like the professorial gadflies of American history who love proving to naïve freshmen that the Founding Fathers owned slaves, coupled with them, smoked marijuana and didn't believe in Calvinism. Clearly, Professor Dart was a Leftist on matters of rain. Can you be right wing on rain? Yes, you would carry an umbrella. He was no Umbrella Man, which by the way, is the title of a pretty interesting Partridge Family song whose lyrics make absolutely no sense: *Umbrella Man, shower me with all your love…*

Here was the myth Professor Dart debunked, straight from his book:

> A common association made by people in other sections of the United States is Oregon and rain. It does rain in Oregon but the annual amount received in the Willamette Valley, the most heavily populated section, is surprisingly modest and half of the state has a decided water deficit. How did such an ugly rumor get started (and if you belong to the James G. Blaine society, how do we perpetuate it?) and what is its basis in fact? If you have relatives from the east visiting for Christmas vacation they will be convinced that we receive at least 100 inches annually and will not believe the fact that the 40 inches in Portland is less than the yearly average in their home town.

The James G. Blaine Society! Professor Dart! A sly card-carrying member in the first person plural! *We.*

Late in his career, Oregon writer Stewart Holbrook invented the fictitious James G. Blaine Society, named after a non-descript candidate for President, and dedicated to undermining the development of Oregon. Holbrook died in 1964 but in 1971 the organization was incorporated and mounted a satirical campaign to discourage people from moving to Oregon. Their motto was, "Oregonians don't tan; they rust."

I have little doubt Professor Dart was a key member of the modern James G. Blaine Society, perhaps a high priest. I'll bet he spent his entire academic career deliciously debunking the rain myth for his students in Oregon and propagating it to the rest of the nation. He was nothing less than a master spy for his uncreated country of Oregon rain trying to dissuade others from moving here. No wonder I never missed his class.

By the way, our flag is comprised of gray stripes on a gray field and nothing else. And our currency is gorgeous, exquisite little woodcuts of rain with as many drops as the bill's denomination. No words.

NOVEMBER 18, 2012

As I wrote earlier, *Sometimes a Great Notion* is the greatest book on rain in the history of Oregon literature. Currently the greatest, I might add. I'm still writing this book.

Layer upon layer of rain shellacked the cabin late last night and scared Sonny practically under the bed. I don't even think of the cabin as a domicile anymore. It's become more of listening post but I'm listening for friends and fairies, not enemies.

It is impossible to sleep during this kind of storm so I went to the rain section of my library and pulled out Richard Brautigan at random and discovered the greatest short story on rain in the history of Oregon literature. I reprint it here knowing that I am violating various copyright laws. My defense is: rain recognizes no copyrights and rain commanded me to include this story because rain doesn't want readers to forget Richard Brautigan. You know why? Because in one of his poems, "November 24," he wrote, "She's mending her hair with rain" and with that line, Brautigan created an exclusive character of rain you must meet because she will undoubtedly change the world in some small or large wonderful way.

I would do things like that when I was sixteen. I'd hitch-hike fifty miles in the rain to go hunting for the last hours of the day. I'd stand along-side the road with a 30:30 and my thumb out and think nothing of it, expecting to be picked up and I always was.

"Where are you going?"

"Deer hunting."

That meant something in Oregon.

"Get in."

It was raining like hell when I got out of the car at the top of the ridge. The driver couldn't believe it. I saw a draw half-full of trees, sloping down into a valley obscured by rain mist. I hadn't the slightest idea where the valley led to. I'd never been there before and I didn't care.

"Where are you going?" the driver said, hardly believing that I was get-ting out of the car in the rain.

"Down there."

When he drove off I was alone in the mountains and that was how I wanted it to be. I was waterproofed from head to toe and had some candy bars in my pocket.

I walked down through the trees, trying to kick a deer out of the dry thickets, but it didn't really make any difference if I saw one or not.

I just wanted the awareness of hunting. The thought of the deer being there was just as good as the deer actually being there. There was nothing stirring in the thickets. I didn't see any sign of a deer or the sign of a bird or the sign of a rabbit or anything.

Sometimes I would just stand there. The trees were dripping. There was only the sign of myself: alone, so I ate a candy bar.

I had no idea of the time. The sky was dark with winter rain. I only had a couple of hours when I started and I could feel that they were at an end and soon it would be night.

I came out of a thicket into a patch of the stumps and a logging road that curved down into the valley. They were new stumps. The trees had been cut sometime that year. Perhaps in the spring. The road curved into the valley.

The rain slackened off, then stopped and a strange kind of silence settled over everything. It was twilight and wouldn't last long.

There was a turn in the logging road and suddenly, without warning, there was a house right there in the middle of my private nowhere. I didn't like it.

There was more of a large shack than anything else with a lot of old cars surrounding it and there was all sorts of logging junk and things you need and then abandon after using.

I didn't want the house to be there. The rain mist lifted and I looked back up the mountain. I'd come down only about half a mile, thinking all the time I was alone.

That was a joke.

There was a window in the house-shack facing up the road toward me. I couldn't see anything in the window. Even thought it was starting to get night, they hadn't turned their lights on yet. I knew there was somebody home because heavy black smoke was coming out the chimney.

As I got closer to the house, the front door slammed open and a kid ran out onto a crude makeshift porch. He didn't have any shoes or a coat on. He was about nine years old and his blond hair was disheveled as if the wind were blowing all the time in his hair.

He looked older than nine and was immediately joined by three sisters who were three, five, and seven. The sisters weren't wearing any shoes either and they didn't have any coats on. The sisters looked older than they were.

The quiet spell of the twilight broke suddenly and it started raining again, but the kids didn't go into the house. They just stood there on the porch, getting all wet and looking at me.

I'll have to admit that I was a strange sight coming down their muddy little road in the middle of God-damn nowhere with darkness coming on and a 30:30 cradled down in my arms, so the night rain wouldn't get in the barrel.

The kids didn't say a word as I walked by. The sisters' hair was unruly like a dwarf witches'. I didn't see their folks. There was no light on in the house.

A Model A truck lay on its side in front of the house. It was next to three empty fifty-gallon oil drums. They didn't have a purpose any more. There were some odd pieces of rusty cable. A yellow dog came out and stared at me.

I didn't say a word in my passing. The kids were soaking wet now. They huddled together in silence on the porch. I had no reason to believe that there was anything more to life than this.

NOVEMBER ? 2012

Random rainy thoughts:

No one walking the neighborhood this morning. No one walking the beach either.

The weathermen predict two inches of rain today. Right now, I stare out the window of the Sandbar and see rain blowing parallel to the red neon. Amanda is behind me, talking intelligently about football while I write about rain. Everyone can't believe Oregon lost to Stanford in overtime. Luckily, vodka for breakfast eases the suffering. As one longtime Oregon Coast bartender told me years ago, "This is vodka country." Vodka looks like rain. Rain correlates with many things here.

I am always on the lookout for literary contenders for the rain title so I recently read *The Good Rain: Across Time and Terrain in the Pacific Northwest* by Timothy Egan, a journalist I admire mightily.

The book, published in 1990, began with promise: a quote from *Sometimes a Great Notion*. Then Kesey disappears forever and *The Good Rain* doesn't contain a chapter on rain or virtually any writing about rain. If you are going to call your book *The Good Rain*, shouldn't you write about rain? Egan also disparaged my hometown: "Oregon City still looks like Pittsburgh."

I just finished a distressing biography of Kurt Vonnegut and learned that his older brother Bernard was an atmospheric scientist for General Electric. Bernard holds the dubious distinction of being one of the first scientists to experiment seeding clouds with silver iodide to make it rain. Doubtless the Pentagon caught wind of Vonnegut's research during the Cold War and conspired to turn rain into some kind of weapon against the Soviet Union, whereby torrential rain destroys their grain, which means no vodka, which means the Russia people revolt and the totalitarian regime collapses, which means we win.

Cogitate that evil notion: a defense contract for rain. I would love to believe that various shamanistic approaches of making it rain conjured by the naked holy rain men met with a higher success rate than white coats and silver iodide.

We may get two inches today. Perhaps the weathermen predicted accurately. I really don't care. I've moved well beyond measuring rain with math. There's so much more to it.

At the grocery store, I stood in the checkout line behind three soaked fat men, with sideburns, clearly tourists, buying up all the Hostess products after news of the company's demise hit. They were selling fast all over the nation and sealed boxes of Twinkies were going for $50 on e-Bay. These men carried umbrellas.

I just finished reading a fascinating essay by Umberto Eco, "The Beauty of the Flame," on the significance of fire in medieval literature. Fire was a creator, a destroyer and an avenger in these works, most of which I have never read nor will ever read because they despise nature and sex. Apparently, back then, rain was never seriously discussed in literature, but envision our contemporary world if people had taken up the matriarchal nurturing rain as the central metaphor in Western culture instead of the punishing patriarchal fire. You just know the Papacy would have been long gone by now and the Olympic Games would feature some sort of monument to the eternal rain.

Writing about fire doesn't interest me, particularly when a terrific rainstorm shakes the cabin and brings down branches. Nevertheless, Eco's subheads that divide the essay intrigue me as writing prompts, so I will substitute "rain" for "fire" and respond in rhythm with the falling rain.

Rain as a Divine Element
Especially when it twists and shouts. That's when hypnotism strikes.

Hellrain
Noah felt it. God told him it was coming and how to survive. I have never felt a Hellrain, although I wouldn't mind playing the accordion in a rock band with that name.

Alchemical Rain
…is a primitive sensual magic that most people unknowingly amputated from their lives as soon as they became adults.

Rain as the Origin of Art
Is this the story of my creative life? I hadn't written a word for publication until I drank undistilled rain straight from the bottle. Since I became a drunk, I've written a thousand articles and a dozen books.

Rain as an Epiphanic Experience
My generic baptism into the Church of Christ at the age of ten was the antithesis of epiphany. I wore a strange plastic outfit as lukewarm water attempted to drown my intuition forever.

Regenerating Rain
Rain constantly regenerates and apportions itself to anyone who desires a taste. It never burns out like fire.

All of this reading about fire brings to mind my recent teaching of *The Crucible*. By definition, a crucible is a container that can withstand intense heat. It also is a severe test.

What is the crucible of rain? What trial does rain pose? Is that what this book is about?

I think about those questions as I take a walk in rain that has now become a storm. In the neighborhood, I encounter downed trees, toppled gnomes and linemen clad in orange who work languidly on ladders. As I contemplate the crucible of rain, I also consider David Duncan, author of the third best book on rain in the history of Oregon literature, *The River Why*. When Duncan left the Oregon Coast for Montana some years ago, he became a decidedly different and less compelling writer. He abandoned rain and something went out of him. The spell was broken.

If I leave the Oregon Coast, will that happen to me? Would I even know it?

NOVEMBER 20a, 2012

Drinking black coffee on a day off from work. Rain canceled school. I love knowing I am writing on rain because rain temporarily suspended my job. Is there a correlation?

I watch rain splatter on big sheets of window glass I installed on the deck as some kind of amorphous experiment in photography. In another vague experiment, I also set out a dozen shot glasses on the deck's railing to collect the juice for imbibing later. Rain is moving in monochrome across the sky and I think about REM when REM was very much an elliptical band of rain, but then started making hits, videos and articulating their lyrics.

In their memorably obscure song called "Cuyahoga," about the river that erupted in fire, a line goes: *Let's put our heads together and start a new country up.*

I did that with rain. Anyone can join this country, the Rainlands, if you just cross the boundary-less border, which resembles a billowing curtain of gray wool and not a chain link fence with razor wire. As Henry Miller might say, "It is a country of enchantment which the poets have staked out and which they alone may lay claim to."

As I wrote before, we issue our own currency. We also have created some interesting organizations, competitions, affiliations, offices, distinctions and awards that have no formal processes or regular schedules. They just happen when they happen, meet when they meet, and people instantly belong to them, knowingly or not.

Rain Appreciation Society
First Team All Rain
Rain Hall of Fame
Order of Meritorious Existential Service in Rain
Medal of Rain
Umbrella Eradication Project
Captain of the Clouds
A doctorate in rain conferred by The Institute of Rain
Citizens for Better Sex in Rain
Rain Love Prize
The Whiskey and Rain Advocates
League of Wet Dogs
Rain Czar
The Rainologists
Duke of Rain
Circle of Gray
Center for Rain Centrality
The War on Sun
Legion of Rain
Rain Pornography Enthusiasts
Rainmakers of the Mind
Sustainable Rain Initiative
Union of Rain Strippers
Naked Riders of Rain
Perpetual Wet T-shirt Contest

Order of Rainy Day Women
United Soviet of Rain
Miss Rain
Rain Mobilization Committee
Live Rust
Fellowship of Rain
The Masters of Rain
Monochrome Adventure Club
The Storm Guild
Rain Anonymous

NOVEMBER 20b, 2012

It had rained nearly four inches in 24 hours. Portland weathermen had gone deep into their online thesauruses and blow dryers for novel and moronic adjectives (wicked) to anthropomorphize a routine coastal storm.

Did you know that the famous crime novelist Elmore Leonard cautioned aspiring writers to never use the word "suddenly" in fiction when something dramatic instantly occurs? He said it was pure cliché, amateurish.

Nevertheless, this is a romance story in rain so….

SUDDENLY I felt a call to visit the beach.

Yes, I hear that call four times a day, but this sound was different, new, original, sort of like hearing *Sgt. Pepper* for the first time even though the album is nearing 50 years old.

I loaded Sonny into the truck and we headed to the beach. Overhead, white gulls followed us in a gray, black sky.

We hit the sand and rain peppered us like a spread from a shotgun blast. Waves rolled a hearty brown and blue and sea foam scurried north down the sand, piling up here and there. Bubbles shimmied for seconds and then the glancing rain broke them apart in dignified silence.

Sonny and I cruised south and then I saw her, 50 yards away, looking out to the ocean, tilting toward the jetty. Even from afar she appeared gorgeous as only antediluvian things washed ashore can appear. I moved toward her, wondering what I might say, wondering if she would deign to converse with me. That is, if she spoke English, which I desperately hoped she did not. I didn't want to hear her speak the debased language of politicians and reality TV stars with alleged coloring from a phony sun.

Sonny didn't follow me. My dog was more interested in canine messages deposited at the wrack line.

She was lying down with the lower part of her torso obscured by sand and kelp. I saw no legs.

I greeted her, she nodded, winked and tossed back her long hair, which was colored a dark grayish green. She wore no makeup unless you count the jagged lines of salt that etched her face. I had difficulty concentrating because of her exquisite beauty and the fact that she wasn't wearing any clothes. She never said a word but we communicated nonetheless. Rain is like that. As it turns out, her least favorite word is *whatever*, she has no need for a smart phone, and loathes the oil industry for its despoiling ways. She's also bored with overly aggrieved fishermen with their boat loads of Freudian defense mechanisms, the chief one being compensation.

At one point, she smiled and gestured toward my camera stuffed halfway in the pocket of my pea coat.

I caught her drift.

She was an excellent model and taught me a thing or two about the photographic uses of sea foam and rain.

An hour later, I had a date for a picnic on the rocks at Boiler Bay. I'd bring kelp and vodka. She was bringing fresh rain, shot glasses, mussels and a flute crafted from the horn of an ancient narwhal.

Her name? I wish I could pronounce it. It sounded vaguely Nordic.

NOVEMBER 21, 2012

This morning, Sonny and I ventured to the beach. Gulls and a lone ranger of a pelican patrolled the wrack line. Precipitation had quit falling but the air felt freighted with rain, like a mighty collapse was imminent, like little black Bibles might fall from the clouds. There was one tiny porthole open to the sun. I didn't see another human for miles and that made me happy. I could feast alone on, "The salt air loaded with cream for our breathing," as the poet Richard Hugo wrote. Hugo was a great poet on rain, the ocean and taverns too.

The porthole slammed instantly shut and rain found us. Then sleet, then hail. The fight was on. I was in the ring taking stinging jabs to the face and body. What do you do in the ring against a heavyweight rain? When you can't run and can't hide?

You go Ali against Foreman. You cover up and go rope-a-dope. Rain will exhaust itself and then you spring from a sweaty clench, fling your arms open and...not punch back.

You never box rain. It is never your opponent. Knowing that is the only way to win.

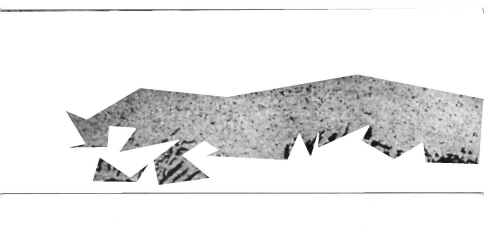

RAIN: a love story

A POETIC CONFRONTATION

On a Thursday in late November 2010, a month that eventually produced the second wettest November since instruments have measured depressing records of this kind, I sat at my desk in my classroom and heard rain falling for the 31st day in a row. I immediately thought of one of Ken Kesey's enduring riffs about rain from *Sometimes a Great Notion*: "...there is solace and certain stoical peace in blaming everything on the rain, and then blaming something as uncontrollable as the rain on something as indifferent as the Arm of the Lord."

True enough. But not true enough for us to survive. Blaming gets you nowhere with rain.

That morning, my patience with rain hung by the thinnest of beaded cobwebs as I schemed how to motivate my listless and intellectually waterlogged students. Soon, they would start streaming in with pale, vacant faces resembling prisoners of war, moisture steaming from their clothing. I suspected many of them had gone insane.

We've got to move into the deluge, I thought. *It's the only way to shatter the stasis.* Last year, I had employed a similar strategy with the photography class and the resulting black and white photographs of rain they took around campus in 30 minutes revolutionized our thinking about the beauty of rain. I had made up the lesson on the spot and forced them (and myself) to examine rain with a camera on a tight deadline. By the end of the slide show that culminated the assignment, all students were converted into a love cult of rain that I also made up on the spot.

In trudged the creative writing students with their soggy frowns. In recent weeks their angst had secreted like pus from a lanced boil. On the whiteboard in huge black words I wrote the fatal statistics: 19 inches of rain had fallen during the last 30 days, seven the last 72 hours, four since midnight, even heavier rain was forecast for the next couple of days, records were going to be shattered, the county was already underwater, rivers were running well above flood stage but had yet to crest, school might be cancelled for a week, and there was only one thing we could possibly do: *go into it, right now.*

The students gave me a big whatever. They were in worse condition than I imagined. I climbed on a desk and yelled, "We're going to confront rain and poetry is our method! Are you with me?"

Whatever began to dissipate, slightly, visibly, sort of like condensation.

I jumped off the desk and told the class to get paper, pen and drain the pus. We were traveling to a new country called the Rainlands and abandoning clichés and complainers. I wrote a prompt on the board and everyone quickly responded with one word or phrase. Then I threw out another one. I asked the students to assist me and several volunteered prompts. Some 15 minutes later we had written on the following:

1. What magic can you perform with rain?
2. Describe your favorite kind of rain.
3. Make a case for or against using an umbrella.
4. Concoct a love potion that has rain as an ingredient.
5. Blame something on rain.
6. Complete this simile: Oregon rain is like_____.
7. What do politicians do with rain?
8. Devise a slogan and sketch a logo for Oregon rain.
9. Pluvial or petrichor?
10. You overhear a tourist say how much she hates rain. How do you respond?
11. Make a case for the greatest song about rain.
12. Defend your preference: running naked in Oregon rain or tanning on a tropical beach.
13. What can you hear if you listen to rain?
14. Rain = _____.
15. Rain helps me understand...
16. What type of rain are you? Construct a rain metaphor for yourself.

It was time for confrontation, to blast a bazooka round into the congealed void of *whatever*.

"We're now going outside in rain. Leave your stuff here. Spread out across the football field so you're at least 50 feet away from another student. Tilt your face toward the sky, close your eyes, open your mouth, taste rain for 30 seconds, and then get back to class."

I led the charge out the door and 41 students followed me into one of the heaviest rains I have ever witnessed in my life. One boy took off his shirt. One girl started to, but I stopped her just in time. We aren't quite there as a culture—yet.

Back in class five minutes later, I had the students delete, add, edit and rearrange their responses to construct a poem. Ten minutes later, I asked for readers. I'll never forget Logan's poem:

> Every November, the Oregon cult
> goes to work.
> We quarry up each raindrop
> to use as our limestones
> to construct a great church
> to the giver of Oregon's purpose.

NOVEMBER 22, 2012

It occurs to me that no one has made the greatest film on rain in the history of Oregon cinema. In fact, someone has made the worst film on rain in the history of Oregon cinema and his name was Paul Newman. The movie, *Sometimes a Great Notion*, was filmed on the Oregon Coast during the summer of 1970. That was Newman's first mistake. You can't make a great film on Oregon rain in the summer. As it turned out, all rain in the movie was utterly fake. Kesey must have been aghast when he saw it.

NOVEMBER 24, 2012

I recline in bed and drink a mediocre scotch while reading a lifeless contemporary novel set in Western Oregon that has yet to mention rain. Is it possible that someone wrote a novel set in Western Oregon that doesn't include rain? If he did, I would equate it to writing a novel set on the moon and not writing about the moon.

Rain juices down from the sky and I start thinking of scotch, single malt scotch, whisky versus whiskey, scotch on the rocks, scotch neat, scotch and soda, scotch and rain, scotch and Kesey, scotch mist, the Bay City Rollers, the Highlands, the Lowlands, the classic whisky movie *Whisky Galore* and Robert Burns. Something mysterious far, far away from a distant land of rain is calling me through rain.

I get up, carry the scotch into the living room and Google "scotch mist and rain" on the typewriter. I scroll down the offerings until something grips me: The Rain Museum (http://rainmuseum.net/) I enter and read:

> Rain is inextricably linked to our lives…Rain at times even seems to secretly govern the emotional life of our societies. The Rain Museum is the world's first institution to celebrate this overlooked and euphoric phenomenon.

Rain plays a part in all our cultural life and delivers a powerful narrative device that is used in film, literature, art and music. The impossibility to escape rain is a metaphor for human vulnerability, and when we end up being totally drenched by a real downpour, we are reminded of how we have to accept the fact that fate soaks us relentlessly.

In literature, film or music heavy rain often corresponds to a heavy outbreak of feeling in the hearts of the protagonists. They might not even be aware of it, but in front of the backdrop of rain they fall in love, fall out of love, hate each other, or scream to the soundtrack of rain beating down on the tin roof.

Interestingly, the country that is generally viewed as the Empire of Rain simultaneously stands for a culture of emotional repression. It seems ironic that the image of Great Britain as the country of rain and umbrella stands in dialectical opposition to the fact that nowhere else feelings are so meticulously hidden as in this wet country.

Three hours later I exit the Rain Museum and its many pleasant digressions. I take a belt of scotch and recall rain in the country of umbrellas and corned beef. I spent a winter month in London once, drinking tea and not writing. Rain was formidably benign there.

Who are these curators of England's rain? It looks like I have some stolid allies for my obsession. This unnerves and challenges me. I prefer to work alone. Rain has a way of doing that to a person.

Not that I ever emotionally repress either, and how ludicrous to think rain secretly governs my emotional life.

NOVEMBER 25, 2012

It was raining translucent silver walls as I drove to Manzanita to make a presentation unrelated to rain that I knew I would eventually bring around to rain nonetheless.

Drivers, every one of them male, were taking ridiculous risks on the highway. I loathed their big trucks and felt sorry for the deer and humans who might suffer because of misplaced impotency and a flaccid mind. Don't defame rain for their masculine vehicular homicide. Rain is all woman.

With the windshield wipers slapping time and someone singing the grays, I sensed I had become Oregon's foremost authority on rain despite the fact that my expertise has nothing to do with metrological prediction and everything to do with aesthetic addiction.

Bob Seger's "Night Moves" played on the radio. It occurred to me that if you set the song during a winter on the Oregon Coast instead of a Midwestern summer, and repeatedly replaced the word "night" with "rain," and changed "cornfield" to "beach," you would almost have the perfect sexy song about rain.

I decided to stop in Lincoln City and visit Pacific Coast Books and talk with Don, an outstanding bookman who is always trying to sell me a signed first edition of *Sometimes a Great Notion* for a mere $250. Perhaps this was the day.

The truck halted in a lake across the street from the bookstore. I got out and prepared for the race: the World Championship 50-meter Sprint in Sideways Rain, a unique track and field event that unfolds a million times a day when it rains sideways on the Oregon Coast.

Everyone who competes, wins.

I leaned into the blocks and saw the finish line at the front door. A log truck rambled by and sprayed up a force field of water. I heard the starter's pistol and exploded onto Highway 101.

Inside the store, victorious, I shook out rain and saw a book with an arresting title resting on a table, a book previously unknown to me — *Between Raindrops.*

I quickly learned that *Between Raindrops* is a hardback anthology of poetry produced by six Oregon poets, published in 1985. I opened it at random and discovered Chapter 5, "Miracles of Rain" by Anita Lewisohn Hamm. I read all 20 of Hamm's poems on rain standing in the aisle as steam unfurled from my pea coat. A few choice wet lines:

- I cannot hear what you say for the crashing of rain slanting its spears against the south windows.
- My music, my flowers, my books, do not interest you. I will stir my solitary cup of "instant" and pretend I'm hosting another lover of rain.

- Of weather there are splendored rains: a night rain shimmers with color.
- Rains make blue puddles with dark pencil outline.
- Thunder drums and rain descends.
- Hear the staccato of rain.
- I took the rain into my thoughts.
- Send all roots rain.
- Do we hear a gentle gurgle in the gutters or is it the silent coursing of our own blood?

Don gave me the rain discount and I bought *Between Raindrops* for $10. *Sometimes a Great Notion* could wait. It wasn't going anywhere. Twenty minutes later, I reached the top of Cascade Head and entered a tunnel of suffocating drenched gray. But there was light at the end.

Rain picked up and rivers ran across the roadway. I passed the wildlife refuge where I served as caretaker for a decade but had to leave because I thought a wildlife refuge meant that wildlife enjoy a refuge from humans. I cannot calculate the number of days I hacked blackberries and planted trees in rain during my service there. As a result, I became someone completely different and still don't fully understand what happened to me despite writing a book about the experience. Maybe writing a book about an experience just obfuscates it. I do know that I labored long hours in rain and how many of us can say that besides loggers, lineman and contractors?

Sonny howled; she remembered her madcap adventures on the refuge. We drove to Nestucca Spit, to Bob Straub State Park. It was raining in colossal, ridiculous proportions and no one was there. We sprung to the ocean's edge and I felt an urge to strip all my clothes and dive through rain into the universal basin of all immemorial rainwater where whales reside, practice true democracy, compose music, never boast of their superiority to human beings, and procreate in waves rolling under the surface of the sea.

I'm almost 50 years old yet feel this urge more and more these days. As Walt Whitman wrote in *Leaves of Rain*: "Urge and urge and urge."

Whitman also wrote in *Leaves of Rain*: "A child said, What is the rain? fetching it to me with full hands; How could I answer the child? I do not know what it is any more than he."

After romping down Nestucca Spit through a stinging airborne ablution, Sonny and I took the Three Capes Scenic Loop past the anti-rain capital of the Oregon Coast, the Pelican Pub, with its overrated beer that funds the ongoing sodomy of Pacific City. Last time I checked they had an umbrella stand in the foyer which I urinated in on my previous visit.

A color of dull silver dominated the landscape until I glided into Sandlake and saw the black barn of Cape Lookout looming in the background. I was driving right into it and giddy at the prospect. There might be answers in there.

I arrived in Manzanita and saw a few zombies with umbrellas lurching down the sidewalks while the living paid them no mind. Rain blew me into a Christmas craft fair and I met a woman selling her soap. All proceeds from the sales went to feed an abandoned calf she rescued from a ditch in Tillamook. She named him Lucky. I asked if she made any soap from rain. She answered "no" but I could tell the idea intrigued her. A few seconds later, she told me she intended to make Lucky Rain Soap. I promised I'd sell it at gigs for the rain book and help save a cow. Potentially, it could end up the noblest outcome of anything I'd ever written.

I bought $50 worth of homemade soap on Black Friday and then rain came at me in ways I cannot begin to fathom. During the next 24 hours:

- I met someone who has a daughter named Rain.
- I heard that someone in Oregon distills spirits with rain.
- I met someone who walked better in rain than anyone I'd ever seen.
- I heard about an artist in Rockaway who fills old light bulbs with "vintage" Oregon rain and makes sculptures and mobiles out of them.
- I met someone who wrote a college thesis on rain.
- I learned of the existence of book called, *A Thousand Friends of Rain: New and Selected Poems 1976-1998* by Kim Stafford.
- I heard that David Lee Roth had written an immortal Zen line about rain.
- I bought a mystery novel called *The Rainy City* for a nickel. It's opening sentence was a line by Raymond Chandler, "God help all men on rainy afternoons."
- I got a text message from a producer of a television show filmed in Portland who wanted my advice on rain.
- I heard a legend about a wild coastal man who walks around naked in his back yard, but only when it rains.
- I learned there was something called "Rain Massage."
- I met an owner of a gift shop who said she'd never seen a greeting card with rain as the subject. She was sure they'd make a fortune.

Make a fortune from rain. *Let me repeat that: make a fortune from rain.* What a great notion. It happens all the time with the sun, but golf and herbicides are typically involved. Speaking of golf, it occurs to me that the best times I ever had with my father were playing golf in rain. We preferred playing in rain because that meant we'd rarely see other tandems or foursomes and could hit as many balls as we liked. It also rained when Dad scored his only hole-in-one, a four-iron from 180 yards. I was with him.

We never once used an umbrella on a golf course.

I haven't played golf in 20 years. I gave away my clubs a decade ago. I may have to go back out and play a round, alone, with a couple of blade irons and real woods rescued from a thrift store. But only in rain, like I used to do in my youth in Oregon City, and punch through British Open winds better than any American golfer who has ever played without an umbrella.

Quick trivia question: who is the greatest professional golfer who never used an umbrella during a tournament?

RAIN: a love story

OF WALKING IN RAIN

Any honest accounting of walking in rain should not omit the reason I had to walk.

One Sunday in January 2012, I took a call from someone I loved deeply and thought was deeply in love with me. After I hung up the phone, I had learned through persistent questioning that she was in love with someone else and had been for months. She offered no reason for withholding the truth. She would have never confessed without my solicitation of her honesty, thereby letting me wonder and wander forever thanks to her silent eternal *whatever*.

It was turning black outside and for some reason I tapped on the bedroom window. It was almost if I was trying to get the attention of someone, but of course nothing was out there except rain, moving like a phalanx across the yard, threatening to collapse a wooden fence. I tapped the window again and realized that I was completely crushed in a way I had never felt before; I had never seen this coming and was shocked and depressed by how my intuition had betrayed me. At this moment, I didn't know anything relevant about myself or love in the world. And in 12 hours, I had to go teach teenagers, model behavior and dispense wisdom.

At first I asked myself, "How did it come to this?" which is the dumbest question in the universe. If you ask it then you already know the reasons why.

I knew the reasons. The story now, however, was not about recreating the past, like Gatsby, but how to advance, always advance, and learn new lessons and a new path. I had no interest in recrimination nor was there any time for it.

That afternoon, rain called to me in a way I had never heard before. It was a recruiting pitch and I enlisted into a leaderless and mysterious organization of rain. I left my room, donned the pea coat and stocking cap, gave Sonny a pat on the head, and walked directly into the phalanx. I knew a discovery of the utmost importance awaited me out there. "One must go oneself to know the truth," wrote Peter Matthiessen in *The Snow Leopard*, perhaps the most influential book I have ever read. In his remarkable journey of personal discovery and healing, Matthiessen had the Himalayan Mountains; I had Oregon rain.

I walked a loop around the neighborhood, down to the beach, and back to the cabin. I repeated the loop three times, something like 10 miles. The last few were in pitch darkness. I did the same thing the next night and the night after that. It rained 4.65 inches in 24 hours on one of those days and I felt rain then like never before.

During these initial walks, I tried emptying my mind by contemplating a koan I devised: "Rain falls everywhere—why not here?" I utterly failed at emptying anything and just kept walking and thinking. This went on for about a month. I never ran, used a flashlight or listened to music on my walks. I virtually never slept. I never once considered talking about it with anyone else. Rain and I talked. Did you know, by the way, that if you talk to rain it will never reply with stock answers dished up from the dictionary of therapy?

One morning at school, I stood facing the whiteboard with a black marker in my hand. Behind me, 37 seniors in my English class watched me prepare to demonstrate a pre-writing process I call "stream of consciousness outlining." I encourage students to try this spontaneous activity prior to beginning their personal research essay, a 2000-word "descent into one's self" assignment where they assay the ultimate exploratory question of their lives.

The process begins by the student writing the personal subject he wants to explore on a large piece of butcher paper. In some cases, the word might be, "divorce" or "depression" or "sexual abuse." The student begins writing or drawing anything related to the subject that comes to mind. If it rolls out with linearity, fine. If not, so be it. Follow the tangents. Just don't stop, don't block, and keep talking to yourself aloud during the process. The ultimate question may emerge, or it may not.

I wrote the word "rain" in block letters. Then I started manically sketching rain, trying to render all the manic ways it falls on the Oregon Coast. Questions came next: what is rain? Why do I love it? What happens if you only drink rainwater? What does rain do to people here? Who was she? I started singing Creedence Clearwater Revival's "Who'll Stop the Rain?" and scribbling lyrics from rain songs. I grabbed blue, green and purple markers and went Jackson Pollock on the whiteboard.

This went on for three minutes and then I stopped, stepped back, stepped forward, and wrote my research question: "What happens when you walk in rain?"

A year later, this book completes the assaying of that question. I don't necessarily recommend walking in rain as a method to write a book. I do think, however, others could benefit from attempting it as an inexpensive, drug-free, means of personal and metrological discovery. Obviously, it works best at the Oregon Coast during winter. My timing was perfect.

At some point, I no longer felt the need to walk at night anymore, although there was still a lot more of walking in rain to come. That will never stop as long as I live. I probably will die that way.

I never saw nor talked to her again. I also never issued her a rain check.

NOVEMBER 26, 2012

Yesterday, I returned the seniors' essays written on the prompt of "My Crucible." They all received A's because their writing was honest, unpretentious, probing, error-free, instructive and didn't contain a single cliché.

As the students digested my undecipherable hand-written comments, I heard an interesting rain falling on the roof. It was almost gossiping. Then the sound of rain matured and asked me to ask the students a question, The Question. I thought this a brilliant idea so I told the students to get out a piece a paper and respond to:

The crucible of rain is_____.

- Allowing rain to enshroud you. You need to no longer fear the destructive qualities of rain. Gain the strength the down pour offers to make it through the storm.
- To not let it drench your mind.
- To go into rain when it's storming outside. You have to be okay with getting SOAKED.
- Trying to find the liquid sunshine… finding the fun in rain… finding the life in the dark… staying positive in a downpour…

- Drenched patio furniture, dead wet sprints to the car, and dealing with wet dogs.
- Embracing rain's indefinite power. It doesn't want to be the pariah of the other well-loved elements.
- Making it an integral part of your life while warm and sunny days become a strange nuance.
- Learning how to enjoy it.
- Realizing rain here will never go away.
- Knowing we must go into it. It changes our moods and violently breaks us down. It's cold and careless; it's a test of survival you can pass if you feel it.
- Knowing that it goes away. I rely on it to help me wash away the stress, fear and anxiety. I love that rain, after an absence, makes me excited for its return.
- Congratulating it when it kicks your ass and makes you change.
- Is being able to walk places without getting wet and without playing in it like a child.
- To accept it and live with it and to try to turn it into some thing positive in life.
- Facing it without umbrella or raincoat but also realizing you need to go somewhere.
- Finding it in your heart not to bitch about the weather.
- Handling the weight of your stress with grace.
- Depends on your living conditions. Poor people in poor housing face a different test than affluent people with good roofs.
- Accepting that living in one of the rainiest places on earth means there is nothing you can do about it except learn to love it. I did.
- Letting it pour over you, don't deny it. If you dwell in it long

enough, you will become a part of it. Rain will guide you, it will find you, it will create a home for you, but you must accept it first.

- Learning to love rain and live in it. If you can make it in rain, you can make it anywhere.

NOVEMBER 30, 2012

Rain, rain, come today, come again every day.

Rain worked for me today. It fell in seven unique Oregon directions and no one is impervious to its permeations when that happens.

First period. In the midst of a toxic exchange with a student whose grasp of the truth is slicker than eel snot, I heard rain—and stopped. I was sick of his lies and their metastasizing influence on other students. I think he tans too.

I walked over to the drawer and pulled out the cheap black umbrella occasionally employed in classroom scenarios for comic effect. I didn't really know where this stunt was going. Rain, you know? I'm letting it take me places heretofore unexplored by any Oregon teacher.

The whole class was watching. I went over to him and handed him the umbrella. He took it.

"I want you to leave my room and walk outside into rain and open the umbrella. You're not worthy of rain because all you do is lie and I am finished with your lies. But if you feel like you want to start learning how to tell the truth and remain part of our family, then throw the umbrella away and stand in rain for the rest of the period, or the rest of the day for all I care, until you sense some real truth manifesting within you. Not your phony truth. I think rain is your last hope to become an honest person."

He asked a question and I answered with the definition of "manifesting." He left without saying another word. I looked around the room and I could see the skepticism in the faces of my students.

Thirty seconds later, a shift in them occurred. They got it. Who can stand in rain for an extended length of time and tell lies? Maybe to someone else, but never to yourself.

A pall hung across the room. I could see it like a stratus cloud and I had to obliterate it or else we'd be fogged in the rest of week.

On the table rested dozens of Christmas figurines and candies, props for our holiday photography show.

"Go into rain and get me the greatest Christmas figurine and candy rain shots in the history of commercial photography. I want Christmas aesthetically redefined with rain. Kill the cliché of snow forever!"

A hand shot up with a question and I defined "aesthetically."

They grabbed their cameras and sprinted into diagonal rain. Several fell down in the hall and one was seriously injured, but we splinted the arm and she went on with the assignment.

Thirty minutes later, rain-streaked teenagers returned in a laughing frenzy to show me their shots. I saw soaked Santas, drowning elves, angels showering in downspouts, sleighs dashing though puddles, and silver drops on candy canes. My photographers created fresh metaphors for Christmas. They created a new line of Oregon Christmas cards that could earn us a fortune.

Driving home after school, I chose a mix tape at random. Track one, "No Time" by The Guess Who, plays and a lyric goes, *no time for a gentle rain.*

That lyric about sums up the current state of American K-12 public education. The only time is for standards and testing. By the way, at the behest of the Governor and Oregon's Chief Education Officer, I've written the Standards of Rain for every child in Oregon. Students can easily achieve them. My journalism students just exceeded.

RAIN: a love story

THE HIGHEST ROAD

One morning, Lily burst through the door and winced at the smell of mold that permeated every corner of my classroom. "This is ridiculous!" she yelled and everyone on the journalism staff turned toward her. She had influence. "Look at this school! It's falling apart and I'm getting sick." Behind her, a cascade of water gushed down from the ceiling.

We all agreed. It was ridiculous: rain should not fall inside a school for a month.

It all began in February 2012 when storm after storm threatened to collapse the stained ceiling in the hall outside my Newport High School classroom and, more distressingly, disintegrate the morale of my students. When it rained during school, it rained in my hallway. The custodian set out buckets, totes and garbage cans to catch the mushy tiles, miscellaneous toxic debris and rain, rain, rain.

Unfortunately, his effort proved utterly futile and the teacher across the hall moved out of his room complaining of headaches. Several students went home with migraines and I suffered from the worst bout of insomnia of my life. I couldn't sleep at all so I would arrive at school at 3:45 a.m., burn incense to exorcise the smell of mold, listen to Thelonius Monk, and work on a novel where rain presided in dangerous, infiltrating ways.

One call to the health authorities and I could have shut the entire wing down, but I didn't want to because I was writing like a madman in the moldy mornings and beginning to recognize how rain had exposed the fragility of the educational system and enraged my staff.

They needed to rain themselves, so I let them, rain against the machine. In print.

No one typically asks high school students about the industrial education they receive in preparation to serve the unsustainable American economy built on a house of marked cards. But in February, rain asked my journalism staff loudly and repeatedly, and they began their answer with a manifesto on the cover of a special issue on education:

We the students of NHS,
Deserve to be listened to, understood and require more artistic
opportunities to fill our creative souls.
We demand the expansion of advanced classes outside of the
IB program.

We the students of NHS,
Demand teachers only assign the amount of work
they are willing to grade.
We wonder why it is we leave high school knowing how to write an
analysis of a novel in MLA format, but not how to
balance a checkbook.

We the students of NHS,
Scoff at the stereotypical vapid education plan forced upon us.
We choke on the mathematics and sciences crammed down our
throats, and abhor rigid standards.
We maneuver through tattered plaster and raining ceilings on our
way to academic achievement.

We the students of NHS,
Believe in school spirit.
We will sit gladly on the fake grass outside the sad doors of our build-
ing and see perseverance in our midst.
We would rather have a noisy, cramped education than none at all
because we believe it is our way out.
We will prevail through this disfigured school and come out better than
we were before.
We don't care about the mold on the ceiling
because it will never reach our hearts.
We will strive for what's in and beyond our reach.

We the students of NHS,
Will power through high school, no matter the obstacles, and go on to
accomplish our wildest dreams.

Rain made them rail. Rain sluiced water-washed nuggets of sheer golden expression. No one was opaque or equivocated with their words. No one had time for that with the ceiling falling on their heads and mildew ossifying their minds.

The 20-page issue covered the gamut of educational matters affecting Newport High School students in a forthright and largely first person point of view. The staff wrote on topics ranging from the draconian increase of state testing, terrible cafeteria food, their ideal education, exorbitant cost of college, mediocre teachers, and, most controversially, the reasons why many of them transferred to Newport instead of attending the schools in their home communities. One boy wrote:

> Waldport sucks. I can't think of a good thing about the town—aside from the fact is doesn't take long to leave it. I never attended any Waldport schools but if I had, I'd probably end up a cashier at Ray's. My mom wanted me to receive a better education, so she sent me to Newport High and to shelter me from crazy Good Ol' Boy teachers. Little did she know she was actually exposing me to crazy liberal teachers. Thank you, mom.

Waldport went berserk. There were numerous calls to have me fired and several members of the school board castigated the publication at their monthly public meeting. My principal was hurt by the perceived overall negative tenor of the issue and emotionally addressed the staff with his concerns.

And then an English teacher from nearby Toledo High School sent an email to all personnel in the Lincoln County School District:

> Responsible Adults:

> A student brought to my attention a disturbing article in the Newport High School newspaper. The article I am talking about deals with variances given to Newport High School students and their sometimes slanderous descriptions of Waldport and Toledo High Schools. I do not question the judgement (sic) of the student staff members of the paper, but I do question the judgement (sic) and maturity of the adults who allowed

this type of slanderous vitriol to be included in the otherwise excellent publication. This newspaper was made available to the public at Starbucks, and the apology which needs to follow, also needs to be public (I suggest an open letter in the News Times).Thank you in advance for correcting your lapse in judgement (sic) and doing what is right.

In another email sent to the district he wrote:

On my way home today I stopped by Starbucks and found that the paper was still being distributed to the public. I pulled the remaining issues. Where else is the paper being made available to the public?

When a colleague at another school pointed out to the teacher that removing issues constituted a crime, the criminal wrote back claiming he had a higher moral purpose than the law. You know, like when Rosa Parks rode at the front of the bus.

When I read the staff the emails they wanted blood and castration. I wanted prosecution. An ungrammatical English teacher had challenged my professionalism and stolen our publication.

I talked to my principal and the district superintendent and urged them to call the Newport Police. Here was the relished opportunity to fire a perennial malcontent who couldn't write his way out of a rain-soaked paper bag. The principal and superintendent said they'd look into it. I calmed myself down by walking in rain, but also devised ways of destroying my nemesis. It would have been as easy as rain.

A few days after the staff and I calmed down, my editor, Jennifer, wrote the teacher a letter. I thought it overly tame. I wanted rusty knives, Black Sabbath and disembowelment, but she overruled me:

> We were shocked to learn that you felt the need to remove our paper from one of our distribution sites at the Newport Starbucks.
>
> It hurts to know that our hard work was confiscated due to a few articles you didn't agree with out of the 62 total pieces and 41 photographs contained in the issue. *The Harbor Light* is a student-produced publication. We sell ads to fund it, write it and distribute it ourselves. It comes as a surprise to us that a teacher would denigrate the work produced by students who genuinely care about the product.
>
> Not only were our stories denied the possibility of being read, but our advertisers were deprived the chance of being seen around the community. Advertisers pay good money to gain readership in our issues. We are a business. Your choice to censor our work denied them of their right to be seen, a right that they pay for.
> If you disagree with the content of our student produced publication, we urge you to write a letter to the editor rather than deprive us of our right to be read by members of our own community.
>
> Sincerely,
> Editor in Chief

The teacher never responded.

But we did, and I'll never forget the genesis of our rejoinder.

It was another black morning and I asked the morose staff to gather around me at the front of the classroom to respond to criticism and select a cover story for the next issue. They groaned, sloshed over and looked not-so-discreetly to their cell phones for deliverance.

Spring Break, also known as the Oregon Coast Rain Festival for Tourists, was fast approaching and offered maximum potential to reach new readers, most of whom would be cursing rain in their motel rooms or Starbucks. They'd be busy downloading endless apps on their phones, losing their minds, California dreaming, and unknowingly primed for an education on rain. We would teach them.

I was leading a lackluster discussion when the sound of a thousand staple guns emanated from the roof. I stopped talking; we paused silently and listened to a storm strafe the school. In the hall, a few ceiling tiles crashed to the floor and most of us felt mold spores tickling our nostrils.

Yes. *Yes*. We looked at each other and nodded. Championship teams are like that.

We would bring rain in a way unprecedented in the annals of American magazine journalism or the history of world literature for all we knew. We would make peace with rain, sign a treaty, become editorial allies and counterattack creatively together with such a fluid, gonzo, psychedelic, hard core Oregon masterstroke that our arid industrialized critics wouldn't know what hit them because no one had ever sent ice picks raining down on their steel shore. One of them would undoubtedly land on the Toledo teacher's flaccid pedagogical penis where it might not even inflict pain.

In three weeks we produced *two* separate 12-page publications on the subject of rain, one a guide for locals, the other a guide for tourists. Love and hate. Clarity and misunderstanding. We released them on consecutive days and distributed them to 50 places off campus, including Waldport and Toledo. The publications featured nothing but writing and art about rain. Every photograph in both issues was a heretofore stunning unseen image of rain that unfurled flags of tiny and large metaphors with every viewing. We had stories about mold, gray, umbrellas and how to pick up tourists in rain. We had a short story about a girl who fell in love in rain. I contributed a sermon. We ended the issues with poems.

Erica wrote my favorite piece:

> First, you must forget about the rumor that rain is bad luck. Do you really expect the sun to wash the streets and create rainbows? Rain is a great and beautiful Oregon thing, a living thing, a creature unto itself.

> Second, along with your new understanding of rain, close your umbrella and step out into the rain. Feel the cleanliness of each drop sink into your skin and see the glistening sparkle in every tear falling before you. Whether you believe in magic or not, you will feel yourself absorb the energy of the rain and feel as if your very soul is being cleansed.

> Third, try to create a personal connection with the rain. You may not know it, but deep down, everyone has rapport with

this unpredictable element. Rain contains an uncanny resemblance to our emotions—uncontrollable, yet mystical and completely necessary. You should consider falling rain the greatest asset in your life. But you have to feel it on your face. Looking is not enough.

I bundled the issues for the Toledo teacher and attached a note written on toilet paper. It was curt:

TOP THIS MOTHERFUCKER!

Yours truly,
Slanderous Vitriol (great rock band name, by the way)

I asked Jennifer to read it. She did and scowled. It was her magazine more than mine.

"You taught us to always take the high road Mr. Love," she said. "You told us never to get in the gutter."

Unless it rains, I thought. *Rain flows there to the sea.*

I cut the note without objection and mailed the issues.

We took the highest road and let rain speak for itself.

He never responded. How could he? We won. We let our rain crush him.

DECEMBER 3, 2012

Raina, one of my former prize students at Newport High School is waitressing and comes over to take my order. Her parents named her after rain.

We say "hello" and I get right to the point by asking: rain or sun?

She doesn't delay. "Sun. Rain makes me lazy."

"I can't put that into my book!"

"At least I was honest."

DECEMBER 4, 2012

It rained and blew all last night. I just stared out the window and listened to sounds of ripping weather and the Coast Guard helicopter hovering above the Newport Airport. I wonder what it feels like to fly metal through durable rain?

Rain has fallen all day, never once subsiding since I entered my classroom to the time I'm writing this from my teaching desk nine hours later.

We're looking at a two-inch day for sure, perhaps three, the amount when the joy begins, when you either love the juice or quit the Oregon Coast. I've lost count of all the quitters who quit during my 15 years in residence. One day, they just vanish without a trace, and you never hear from them again because they didn't have the courage to tell the truth. It must be something very debilitating indeed to admit rain defeated you. I've actually never heard anyone say it aloud.

Earlier, the seniors sprinted into second period, and I mean sprinted. They came hydroplaning in from the parking lot trying to protect their essays from the ravages of rain. All their attempts proved futile, even if the students took the precaution of encasing their papers inside Ziploc bags at the bottom of their waterproof backpacks. Which many did.

It is something unique in the annals of public secondary education to receive 40 soggy essays on the subject of rain. We all laughed together at this beautiful absurd synergy. They know I'm writing a weird book about rain and they want to get in the game and eagerly assist. They became positively giddy when I told them to wait for a storm, then find an oddball or perfectly normal-looking person around town, and ask one question, and not an obvious one of the banal television news variety. Ask: what can you do with rain?

DECEMBER ? 2012

Right now…"The wind is sewing with needles of rain." An Oregon poet wrote that immortal line almost a century ago.

"What was restlessness will rain." She also wrote that immortal line, in the greatest poem on rain in the history of Oregon literature.

Where will my restlessness rain? I have tried to answer that question my entire adult life.

The poet also inquires, "What have I given rain?"

I find that the second most penetrating existential question I've ever heard. Number one was asked of me by a dancing grandmother who was drunk in a Newport bar.

It was a dark and stormy night when the question rang out. "Are you in the rock zone?"

I answered, "yes."

"Well," she said, "you look like you belong."

Is there such a place as the "rain zone?" Am I already there? The poem is "Rain" and the poet's name is Hazel Hall. She was a seamstress and poet confined to a wheelchair who lived upstairs in her parents' Northwest Portland home. She never married and died in 1924 at the age of 38.

Again, I am probably violating various copyright laws by including this poem. Again, rain recognizes no copyrights:

> I have raised my hands to rain,
> Raised my hands until my lifting
> Fingers, like warm snow, seemed drifting
> Into rain, becoming rain.
>
> I have given all my hands.
> Rain has taken them and made
> Out of them a liquid shade
> To lay upon a place of sands.
>
> What stirred in my pulse now sighs
> In the long sigh of the rain;
> What was restlessness will rain
> Against some woman's windowpane
> And make a woman close her eyes.
>
> What my fingers had of shape
> Is a curve of blowing light,
> Moving in unhurried flight,
> With the rain, to its escape.

Yet what have I given rain,
Who have felt the edge of rain
Fray my fingers, who have striven
To give much, what have I given
But a little moving pain?

And what have I more, what boast
Of a meaning may I keep,
Who am weary as a sheep
And slightly pleasured like a ghost?

Reading this poem somewhat unnerves me because it forces me to consider something. Is a little moving rain all I have to offer?

DECEMBER 5, 2012

7-DAY FORECAST FOR NEWPORT

Today: A 30 percent chance of showers, mainly before 10am. Mostly cloudy, with a high near 50. Light and variable wind becoming west around 5 mph in the afternoon.

Tonight: Showers likely, mainly after 4am. Mostly cloudy, with a low around 40. Southwest wind 7 to 9 mph. Chance of precipitation is 60%. New precipitation amounts of less than a tenth of an inch possible.

Thursday: Showers. High near 50. Southwest wind 11 to 13 mph, with gusts as high as 21 mph. Chance of precipitation is 80%. New precipitation amounts between a tenth and quarter of an inch possible.

Thursday Night: Showers. Low around 41. West southwest wind 8 to 10 mph. Chance of precipitation is 80%. New precipitation amounts between a tenth and quarter of an inch possible.

Friday: Showers. High near 50. West wind around 10 mph. Chance of precipitation is 80%. New precipitation amounts between a tenth and quarter of an inch possible.

Friday Night: Showers likely. Mostly cloudy, with a low around 39. Chance of precipitation is 60%.

Saturday: A 50 percent chance of showers. Mostly cloudy, with a high near 49.

Saturday Night: A chance of rain. Mostly cloudy, with a low around 36.

Sunday: A chance of rain. Mostly cloudy, with a high near 47.

Sunday Night: A chance of rain. Mostly cloudy, with a low around 37.

Monday: A slight chance of showers. Mostly cloudy, with a high near 51.

Monday Night: A slight chance of showers. Mostly cloudy, with a low around 39.

Tuesday: A chance of rain. Mostly cloudy, with a high near 50.

DECEMBER 6, 2012

Rain counterattacks ferociously at dusk. By nightfall, it has retaken the landscape and dug in deep.

I traverse the Yaquina Bay Bridge, or Green Lady as I call it, in the truck and the gas gauge starts blinking red. I pass several rain men in hoodies walking somewhat bent into the wind. They weather in Oregon Tavern Age (OTA) this way.

The Shell Station glows yellow in rain. I have only a few minutes before the debut of the school play, a murder mystery starring several of my star students. They can expect the loud sound of rain during the show to provide an aural macabre that might elicit a particularly sinister performance by the cast.

One never knows about indoor or outdoor creative public performances in Oregon. Many times they are interrupted and accompanied by a raucous symphony of discordant rain that takes the performances in wild unforeseen ways. It's happened to me a dozen times.

Sheet after sheet slams into the Shell Station. The shelters are a joke.

As much as I worship rain, no one in her right mind would trade the warmth of a vehicle's interior to pump gas in a windy downpour.

And because this is Oregon, one of only two states that still doesn't allow customers to pump their own gas, I never will. The law passed in 1951 and Oregon voters have refused several times to repeal it.

I love talking to Oregonians who pump my gas. I've had many of my best Oregon conversations this way. The attendants always have interesting stories to tell and certainly know more than Google Maps. One needs only to get off the phone, ask and listen.

A Latino man in his 20s blasts through the sheets dressed in day-glo coveralls. I power down the window to greet him and it begins raining into the cab. We say "hello" and I ask him for a fill of regular.

A question instantly comes to me: "What's it like pumping gas in rain?"

He doesn't hesitate. "I wouldn't wish it upon my worst enemy."

"Really?"

"You bet!"

He sprints into the sheets to help another customer and I start searching for a new mix tape consisting of Christmas songs recorded in mono from scratched records. The window goes up.

A few seconds later, a tapping on the glass frightens me. It's the man. I power down the window and rain slaps my face.

"But it beats this!"

He holds up his left hand palm forward and wiggles the stump where his pinky should wave. "I lost this logging in rain. That's a lot worse than pumping gas in rain."

I may have to reassess my premise for this book. I don't want to become a dilettante of rain. Ralph Waldo Emerson said, "A dilettantism in nature is barren and unworthy," which sums up most of Pacific Northwest nature writing the last two decades. A dilettantism in work, however, other people's work, is much, much worse.

DECEMBER 7, 2012

An unforgettable rain slants from the sky, hurling pikes at Oregon's worst enemy, meaning the grasping wastrels of the land. I watch from the deck and the attack begs for an intense visual representation, although what size and medium I cannot say. As I type up notes on this phenomenon, I ask aloud, "What artist has made the greatest piece of art depicting Oregon rain?" I think for a moment as a cannonade of rain resounds through the neighborhood. I think some more. I brew tea and bring it outside. It's too hot to drink so I extend the cup into the storm and hold it there until my cup runneth over.
Tea and rain. I then sip a metaphor.

The answer arrives with the second sip. Frank Boyden, an artist who's lived on Cascade Head for 40 years, has made the greatest piece of art depicting Oregon rain. It's any one of his hundred or thousand etchings of rain. Years ago, I used to own a small one, no larger than a baseball card, and I when I inspected it, which was daily, I sensed it had secret information to impart and that Frank Boyden was a timeless artist of secrets in rain. Only in recent days have I finally understood how this etching influenced me and I vaguely recall it looking like this:

In 2010, on a rainy afternoon dripping with sadness and irretrievable loss, I gave the etching to someone I had slighted. Where in the world does it hang today? Did the gift of Frank's rain absolve me? Doubtful.

DECEMBER 8, 2012

I drove 222 miles in rain to sell seven books and give 13 away. I also sat in rain next to a vagrant and eavesdropped on his conversation with Ken Kesey. He may or may not have known Ken was a statue in downtown Eugene. They were talking about a Grateful Dead show in Oregon from the 1980s and a particularly fine rendition of "Box of Rain." In fact, at one point, the vagrant started singing it.

Ken didn't say anything. I sang harmony and recalled an unforgettable line on rain about the Grateful Dead that Richard Brautigan wrote many years ago:

> The day they busted the Grateful Dead
> rain stormed against San Francisco
> like hot swampy scissors cutting Justice
> into the evil clothes alligators wear.

My event at the library went well. During the question and answer session, an elderly ponytailed man wearing pajamas asked: "What are you working on?"

"A book about rain."

The audience of 40 immediately perked up.

"Are you ever going to write about something modern in Oregon?" He didn't mean it as an insult.

"Isn't rain modern?" I said.
He nodded, as did everyone else. Then they all smiled. A book on rain appeals to every demographic in the region—OTA to OSU, farmer to hipster, vegan to Republican...well at least the Tom McCall Republicans, that nearly extinct political species in Oregon.

I had driven a long way but it was worth the marketing education: rain will sell.

DECEMBER 9, 2012

Cat waits for me after class and hands me a piece of paper and says, "I wrote this up last night listening to rain and thought you might like to read it for your book."

How will I ever quit this job and these special Newport kids? Do teachers in Los Angeles have students give them unsolicited writing about the sun?

> Some nights, when it rains, or is storming outside, I like to lay awake and just listen to rain. It's not so much I believe the rain holds any kind of answer or that I will receive an epiphany from it. I just like the sound. It's a very serene and soothing sound, and is easy on the ears. Listening to rain clears my mind and creates a sense of clarity and cleansing. It has a rhythm like music and instruments that play in unison to harmonize one specific sound. It can change cadence, but the sound is still the same. The rain seems to be the only decisive sound in life sometimes.

"I just like the sound." That might be the most perfectly concise sentence I've ever read about rain.

Is that what this book is really about?

RAIN: a love story

RESCUE

Mist eroded into January dusk as I left my house to walk to the beach and see the day's last light diffusing over the ocean. Sonny stayed behind, exhausted from an earlier ramble down the sand.

Fifty yards from the house, I saw a dark mass moving in the street. I came closer and soon found myself kneeling and petting a runty and rotund black lab with a distinctive white forepaw. She was soaked, gray in the muzzle, well groomed, and without a collar.

Mist turned to rain and then rain turned to a word that English hasn't invented yet.

I know all the dogs in the neighborhood but didn't recognize this one. I couldn't leave a lost dog stranded in heavy rain, so I carried her home because she didn't seem inclined to follow me.

Long ago when I dated the woman I eventually married, a stray dog crossed our path as I drove us to a movie. She told me to pull over but I objected because arriving late to a movie used to rank as my top pet peeve. It was also raining, and at this immature point in my life, I saw rain as an anathema instead of a blessing.

She raised her voice, commanding me to stop. I did. She said, "There are three kinds of people in the world: 1) people who help stray dogs when it's not convenient; 2) people who help stray dogs when it's not convenient and raining; 3) people who never help stray dogs. I only date the second person."

It required considerable effort, but we corralled the dripping dog in the car, and read a phone number on his tag. We drove for what seemed like forever until we found a payphone. She made a call and leave a message. A few hours later, we reunited the dog with its over-joyed owner and celebrated by cooking a fancy Italian meal and going bowling.

Back in the cabin, the lab seemed lethargic, depressed. She refused to eat and fidgeted all night. In the morning, I put her in the fenced back yard with Sonny and drove to work.

During a break between first and second period, I went outside to the parking lot and called animal control for any news of a lost dog in the Newport area. Sure enough, a couple from Vancouver had reported a lost dog, a black lab with a distinctive white forepaw. I got their number and called immediately. While I waited for an answer, the bell rang; I was tardy to my own class! Not to worry because I excused myself. I have a policy that any student who says, "Mr. Love, I was late to class because I was rescuing a stray dog," earns an eternal free pass on future tardies. They need only document the attempt with their phones.

I got a man on the phone. He spoke with a heavy Russian accent and was positively ecstatic. Apparently, the dog was going a bit senile and had wandered away from a beachfront rental a half mile away from my cabin. The couple had searched in vain and then returned to Washington. We ended our conversation by making a plan to meet after school. He was leaving Vancouver in an hour.

Bolting into journalism, I screamed, "I just rescued a dog!" There was some scattered applause and then we went about cranking out another edition of the magazine. During the next break between classes, I went outside into rain and talked to the man's wife, also possessed of a Russian accent. As it turned out, she was driving down with her daughters that afternoon to reclaim the dog.

I walked back inside and told my creative writing students the tale. I then imagined aloud to them that the woman was the wife of a rich Russian mobster, and would come bearing gifts of fine Vodka, caviar, a shiny revolver, and possibly one of her blonde, statuesque daughters.

After lunch, on a lark, I called a neighbor to go check on the dog. She returned my call a few minutes later and said there was no black dog in the yard or in the house, only Sonny. She had escaped! With my teaching concluded for the day, I ran to the truck and raced home to search for the dog.

Speeding down Highway 101, I made a mental count of how many dogs I had rescued and found homes for in my 15 years of living on the Oregon Coast. Seven wins and two losses. Not bad, but not good enough. I wanted an eighth victory.

Two hours later, after searching on foot in a light rain, I found the lab exploring the leafy grounds of the vacation rental she had disappeared from. We strolled back to the cabin and I confined her in the back of the truck with a bone until her owner showed up.

At 4:00 p.m., a sedan pulled in my driveway. I walked out and met the woman and one of her daughters, who was neither blonde nor tall. I opened the truck's tailgate and carried the dog down to the gravel. Upon seeing her owner, she went totally nuts. The woman thanked me repeatedly, gave me a hug, and presented a gift card from Starbuck's. They drove away, I gathered up Sonny, and we went to the beach to celebrate. An hour later, I ordered my first Starbucks latte in 15 years and wrote up the rescue story in my journal. At times I became wistful because I occasionally miss my ex wife and her wonderful influence on me. She taught me many important things in life, including lessons on dogs, food, love and rain.

By the way, the dog's name was Lucky.

DECEMBER 10, 2012

It barely rained on the way to school this morning. I patronized JC Market for some fruit and yogurt and observed all the Latino men in mismatched slickers and boots loading up on drip coffee and donuts before going out to do whatever it is they do in rain. I would say these men represent the public face of work in Oregon's rain: agriculture, logging, road crews, construction and everything else. This country is going somewhere new, and I, for one, am glad I will live to see it. The only thing that stands in the way of this new, better country is the Electoral College.

Before first period began, a girl in journalism said she had a Christmas present for me. She reached into her bag and fished out a cassette tape of *Barry*. Yes, Barry Manilow. It was his 1980 gloriously titled release featuring a tinted photograph of him on the cover wearing a denim shirt unbuttoned to the navel.

She handed me the cassette and I knew immediately without reading the track list that it would have something to do with rain. That's how things unfold these days.

Side one, track three: "I Made it Through the Rain." I'd never heard the song before but knew immediately it was going to be the greatest or most fantastically terrible song about rain in the history of American popular music. The bell rang and I couldn't play it then and there.

Hours later I was driving home in light rain and I pushed the cassette into the player. I already knew "I Made it Through the Rain" would be the first song and I hadn't even cued it up. It was. I cranked it to 11 and the cab shook. Strings, piano, horns, reprises, exuberance, crescendos, camp. You couldn't dance to it but who cared? Barry had recorded the biggest ballad on rain ever recorded and Barry killed it. The chorus went:

> *I made it through the rain*
> *I kept my world protected*
> *I made it through the rain*
> *I kept my point of view*
> *I made it through the rain*
> *And found myself respected*
> *By the others who*
> *Got rained on too*
> *And made it through*

You decide. I have no idea what this song means, especially this verse:

> *We dreamers have our ways*
> *Of facing rainy days*
> *And somehow we survive*
> *We keep the feelings warm*
> *Protect them from the storm*
> *Until our time arrives*

Thirty minutes later I was on the beach with Sonny, admiring rain and the gray ocean, when I abruptly broke into Barry Manilow's "I Made it Through the Rain." I halted, went to my knees, pounded the sand in fury, and cursed. I was Charlton Heston in front of the Statue of Liberty at the conclusion of *Planet of the Apes*. BARRY! YOU FINALLY DID IT! YOU MANIAC!

DECEMBER 11, 2012

The clock struck midnight and clouds partially obscured the moon. I opened the bedroom window to hear drizzle fall. Yes, you can hear this soundless symphony. At least, a few of us can. Sleep began to overtake me and I soon drifted into a lovely dream where the whole world was an uncompetitive creative writing class.

The dream ended abruptly when the class's teacher praised a piece of unreadable meta-fiction. I sat up in bed and remembered a previous thought—rain will sell.

John Steinbeck once wrote, "Any fool can make money."

So I thought: "let's be fools in rain and make it rain cash, like the rappers always rap."

I just knew the marketing pros at the state tourism bureau were already on it with all sorts of fun-filled rain vacation ideas ranging from the family-friendly to the prudery-free. I got up and searched the Internet. I found Travel Oregon:

> Oregon isn't a place you see as much as you do. You can sight-
> see our beautiful coast, volcanic mountains, crystal-clear lakes

and deserts that stretch as far as the eye can see. If you're looking for world-class pinots, some of the best food and craft beer
in the country, epic cycling, kayaking, windsurfing or just about
anything else, look no further.

Nothing whatsoever on rain, anywhere.

I find it so difficult to be a fool alone in Oregon rain, but I'm not adverse
to getting rich.

DECEMBER 12, 2012

According to an American Psychiatric Association Task Force on DSM-IV Diagnostic and Statistical Manual of Mental Disorders:

> There has been a regular temporal relationship between the onset of major depressive episodes and a particular time of the year (e.g., regular appearance of the major depressive episode in the fall or winter). Note: Do not include cases in which there is an obvious effect of seasonal-related psychosocial stressors (e.g., regularly being unemployed or celibate or watching television every winter). Full remissions also occur at a characteristic time of the year (e.g., depression disappears in the spring).

The doctors call it Mood Disorder with Seasonal Pattern, formerly Seasonal Affective Disorder, and I suppose any authentic book about rain in Oregon must consider it in some form or another. I do not suffer from it. Indeed, I recently compared my winter habits with the symptoms from a UK study on Seasonal Pattern and found the reverse was true. I might be a freak of nature.

Symptom	Seasonal Pattern Affect	Matt Love During Rainy Season
Sleep	Sleep More / Difficulty Staying Awake	Disturbed Sleep Early Morning Wakening to Listen to Rain
Energy	Fatigue Often Incapacitating Energy Slump in Afternoon	Increased Energy to Walk and Work
Appetite	Craving for Carbohydrates and Sweet Foods	Loss of Appetite
Weight	Increase	Decrease
Concentration	Difficult to Concentrate Often with Additional Memory Impairment	Superb Concentration With Additional Memory Enhancement
Mood	Low Mood During the Winter, Often Severe Remitting in the Summer	Persistent Creative Mood, Always Severe Remitting in the Summer
Feelings	Sense of Misery, Loss of Self-Esteem; Sometimes Hopelessness and Despair Apathy and Flat Affect (Mood)	Sense of Exaltation, Increase of Self-Esteem; Sometimes of Wonder and Promise Active and Psychedelic Affect (Mood)
Anxiety	Stress and Axiety Common	Absense of Stress, Relaxation Common
Libido	Less Interest in Sex	Heightened Interest in Sex
Social	Irritability, Problems Relating to People Withdrawl and Isolation.	Irritability, Problems Relating to People Withdrawl and Isolation Prefers Canines to Humans

Rain fell like hell today, almost two inches, and it weathered everything it touched, from mountains to people, from the corporeal to the metaphorical, to everything that eventually washes to the sea, which is everything. I call this condition The Weathering. In no way do I believe it unhealthy for me. On the contrary, I tend to augment it whenever I can.

The deluge hit its finest orchestration in the morning and I walked my senior English students right into it to combat Seasonal Pattern the best way I know how after years of clinical trials. By the time we reentered the classroom 20 minutes later, saturated, everyone was smiling, shaking all over, and had composed a haiku about rain without the pedestrian assistance of pen and paper. By doing so, they had turned rain around to a love affair worthy of a poem. True, the affair was ephemeral, but I figured the solidity of love would permeate as it usually does. Love never sleeps. Indifference rusts.

My free method to treat Seasonal Pattern is not, however, on any list of approved treatments covered by insurance conglomerates. It works. I know. Walk into rain and see for yourself.

On my drive home from school, I was thinking of Seasonal Pattern, the permeations of love, the suspected influence of my last name on my existential journey, when I stopped at the South Beach Grocery to buy a newspaper and thus enact my daily tactile routine of a dying hand-held American tradition. At the counter was a white-haired OTA man buying four 24-ounce cans of 24-proof Four Loko malt liquor. He chose the red and green cans for what I can only assume were festive holiday reasons.

He paid his bill in soiled change and walked out into rain that blew like flying anvils. I followed him as far as my truck and watched him crack open a can. He started drinking as he splashed though rivulets in the parking lot. He wore sandals, flared jeans and a prodigious NFL jacket, the Colts I think. A few seconds later, he turned west into a thicket of willows and vanished from sight into a river of rain.

There was no rain story there.

DECEMBER 14, 2012

Four in the morning at school. I can feel this book nearing its finale, but one grand adventure remains: walk to school in a ferocious and heavenly morning rainstorm and narrate my stream of consciousness of the experience into a cassette recorder. Channel rain in analog while drifting in stereo. Ride the snake through the lakes. Meet the hoodied rain people and conduct interviews, wring the stories out of them. They'll talk to me because no one has ever asked them about rain before. Transcribe the recording on the Italian typewriter in one manic vodka-fueled/Charley Parker take and do not edit for clarity. Document the greatest drug free, in-the-moment personal account of walking in rain that exists in the history of world literature. Have I lost my mind? Have I become a genius? Is taking this epic walk all that stands between me and Oregon literary immortality? It is even conceivable that in the future, my daring exploit might become a state educational standard for secondary physical education and writing! I'd easily take that over the Nobel Prize in Literature although I would have to continue teaching, which is surely all right by me. There are many more unknown rain lessons out there, waiting to fall on me.

Approximate distance to school: five miles. Approximate length of time: two hours. Attire: blue velour pants, purple Western shirt, pea coat, black waterproof Danner boots, Mr. Chips satchel, Polaroid camera slung around the neck and wristwatch.

I might go tomorrow.[1]

---

[1] I did in fact, walk to school during a rainstorm and met several Rain Creatures along the way. About halfway through my journey, I realized that a stream-of-conscious narrative wouldn't adequately convey the primal nature of the experience. Thus, I pulled out my handy-dandy point and shoot digital camera, started shooting video, and fancied myself as Werner Herzog. To view my short film, visit nestuccaspit-press.com.

DECEMBER 15, 2012

The news of the Newtown Massacre reached me in rain. It feels irrelevant to write about rain today or any day for that matter. But I will write again soon and let the story play out, whatever that story is. All I can say now is that not enough people in my sick country listen to rain, or even know how.

DECEMBER 16a, 2012

7-DAY FORECAST IN NEWPORT

Today: Rain, with thunderstorms also possible after 4pm. Some of the storms could produce heavy rainfall. High near 49. Windy, with a south wind 20 to 30 mph increasing to 36 to 46 mph. Winds could gust as high as 70 mph. Chance of precipitation is 100%. New rainfall amounts between three quarters and one inch possible.

Tonight: Showers and possibly a thunderstorm. Some of the storms could produce heavy rainfall. Steady temperature around 48. Windy, with a south wind 34 to 40 mph, with gusts as high as 65 mph. Chance of precipitation is 90%. New rainfall amounts between three quarters and one inch possible.

Monday: Showers. Temperature falling to around 42 by 5pm. Windy, with a west wind 26 to 33 mph, with gusts as high as 55 mph. Chance of precipitation is 100%. New precipitation amounts between a quarter and half of an inch possible.

Monday Night: Showers. Low around 37. West wind 15 to 20 mph, with gusts as high as 32 mph. Chance of precipitation is 90%. New precipitation amounts between a quarter and half of an inch possible.

Tuesday: Occasional showers. High near 43. West wind around 14 mph, with gusts as high as 21 mph. Chance of precipitation is 90%. New precipitation amounts between a tenth and quarter of an inch possible.

Tuesday Night: A 50 percent chance of rain. Cloudy, with a low around 38.

Wednesday: Rain likely. Cloudy, with a high near 46. Chance of precipitation is 70%.

Wednesday Night: Rain. Cloudy, with a low around 40. Breezy.

Thursday: Rain. Cloudy, with a high near 48.

Thursday Night: Rain. Mostly cloudy, with a low around 40.

Friday Rain: likely. Cloudy, with a high near 47.

Friday Night: Showers likely. Mostly cloudy, with a low around 42.

Saturday: Showers. Mostly cloudy, with a high near 48.

DECEMBER 16b, 2012

Rain has fallen 18 consecutive days. Observations abound as rain penetrates my consciousness and moves in mischievous ways. Rain also moves my body in tantalizing directions.

Two months ago, about the time I started writing this book, Sonny began exclusively drinking water from a bucket in the back yard that collects rainwater. She refuses to drink tap water from her bowl. I am not making this up. I have witnesses.

Yesterday, I saw a bearded OTA man driving down Highway 101 in a 1970s Datsun pickup that sported no paint, only rust. The windshield wipers worked perfectly fine as a staggering rain fell. Unfortunately, the truck had no front windshield. I quickly turned around and chased the truck because I knew its driver was one of the great Oregon rainfreaks of all time and could teach me new skills and sensations. How did I know? He was smiling.

A few miles later, I lost him in rain and wonder if I'll ever meet this holy man.

A real typewritten letter arrived yesterday:

Dear Mr. Love:

I just read that you are working on a book about the rain. I'm writing to encourage you to get on the rain book and have included a sample of my writing to support what you are doing. People talk about being "snowbirds" and going to Arizona in the winter to get away from the rain. I'm a rainbird, and my spirit soars when I can listen to the rain and smell the sweetness it brings.

I really liked the newspaper on rain by the high school students. All of the articles are great fun, and I read the entire issue twice a year. Good job!

Now get back on the rain book and quit reading your fan mail.

"The Dance of Rain" by an Oregonian

I like listening to the rain. I remember being a teenager, staying at my Mom's cousin's house in Seattle, and sleeping in their loft bedroom that had some kind of glass ceiling. I loved listening to the rain on that ceiling—it was such a beautiful, soothing and calming sound. The cousin would yell upstairs "What are you doing?" and I'd respond "nothing." Of course then she would think I was up to no good, run up the stairs, and realize I really WAS doing nothing, just listening to the rain. I'd explain I was listening to the rain and she would think I was nuts and quiz me about what I was really doing. I never convinced her I wasn't plotting some evil scheme, but I was very content to be in that loft, listening to the rain.

Sincerely,
An Oregonian

In all musical genres, virtually every band or solo performer seems to have a song about rain, even rap, even Madonna, even heavy metal, and of course Tom Petty. Songs about rain fall in as many directions as Oregon rain falls. No other subject in music has provided such diversity—not even love. Generally, songs about rain intrigue listeners and avoid clichés. Interestingly enough, many songs about rain have become clichés. It pains me to say this because the Rolling Stones are my favorite rock band of all time, but I consider "Rain Fall Down" from *The Bigger Bang* the worst song about rain I have ever heard. Mick croons:

> *And the rain fell down*
> *On the cold hard ground*
> *And the phone kept ringing*
> *And we made sweet love*
> *And we made sweet love*

Not sexy at all. Maybe if Keith was singing it like he did on "You Got the Silver."

Thankfully, other musicians did rain justice.

Eddie Rabbit loves a rainy night. Buddy Holly agonizes over the raining in his heart. The Beta Band wants to dry the rain. Luke Bryan explains that rain makes corn, corn makes whiskey, whiskey makes his baby feel a little frisky. Dion walks in rain, tears falling, and feels the pain of wishing she was there to end his misery. Neil Young becomes rain he remembers falling. Bruce Springsteen confides that all he loves is the wind and rain. Tom Waits complains that everywhere he goes it rains on him. Lightnin' Hopkins predicts that if it keeps on raining, lightning can't make no time. Lucinda Williams knows that once rain falls down it can't be put back in the sky, so please don't cry about it. She also knows that rain turns dirt into mud, warm and messy, just like love.

Lucinda's rain lines come from the song "Are You Down?"

Are you down with rain? Is that what this book is all about? Who is down? Who is not?

Who wants to even meet, much less know, people who are not down with rain?

The Beatles in "Rain":

> *Everything's the same.*
> *(When the rain comes down.)*
> *I can show you, I can show you.*
> *Rain, I don't mind.*
> *If the rain comes they run and hide their heads.*
> *They might as well be dead.*

The Who in "Love, Reign O'er Me":

> *Only love can make it rain*
> *The way the beach is kissed by the sea*
> *Only love can make it rain*
> *Like the sweat of lovers layin' in the fields*
> *Love, reign o'er me*
> *Love, reign o'er me*
> *Rain on me, rain on me*
> *Only love can bring the rain*
> *That makes you yearn to the sky*
> *Only love can bring the rain*

That falls like tears from on high

Now we come to the most captivating song about rain, "Box of Rain," by the Grateful Dead:

> *Walk into splintered sunlight,*
> *inch your way through dead dreams to another land.*
> *Maybe you're tired and broken,*
> *your tongue is twisted with words half spoken and thoughts unclear.*
> *What do you want me to do, to do for you to see you through?*
> *A box of rain will ease the pain, and love will see you through.*
> *Just a box of rain, wind and water,*
> *believe it if you need it, if you don't, just pass it on.*
> *Sun and shower, wind and rain,*
> *in and out the window like a moth before a flame.*
> *And it's just a box of rain, I don't know who put it there,*
> *believe it if you need it, or leave it if you dare.*
> *And it's just a box of rain, or a ribbon for your hair;*
> *such a long long time to be gone, and a short time to be there.*

I believe people should open a box of rain at least once in their lives and walk into splintered rainlight.

A few days ago, I saw a beautiful Salvation Army bell ringer and watched her interact with shoppers in rain. She stood smiling and dancing in front of JC Market as rain enveloped her. It surely ranked as one of the best displays of positive rain energy in the history or rain. She wore the rain like a ribbon in her hair; she'd obviously opened the box.

Later that day, I paid a quarter for a paperback book at a Waldport thrift store: *Erotica From Penthouse,* published in 1990. One glance at the cover and I just knew this collection of personal narratives would contain at least one, if not multiple, titillating tales of sex in rain. It had to. Perusing the table of contents further fortified my belief:

Are Women Too Easy?
Our First Vibrator
The Indelible Affair
Swan Song Sex
Sex During Divorce
Morning Becomes Erection
Dial S for Sex
Sex in the Dark
Fantasy Game
Steam Heat
I Was a Coke Whore
I Slept With a Gangster
Lesbian Express
The Lesbian Who Loved Men
The Stuntwoman: High Sensation Seeker
The Woman Who Craved Cunnilingus
Sushi Sex
Fear of Lesbianism
A Gismo Named Desire
Foaming at the Mouth
If It's Midnight, It Must Be Jerri
The Erotic Confessions of a Romantic Writer
I Fall For Bastards
Lousy Lovers: A Repair Manual
The Professor of Sex
The Deflowering of a Lesbian Stripper

Single Swing Clubs Hardly Swing
The Family Mistress
The Virgin and the Stowaway
The Castaway and the Prostitute
First Intercourse, 1946
Perversity in Every Port
One Night in Bangkok

I read the entire book at home in one setting while rain grinded hard across the roof and worked its way slowly down the supple shaft of the gutters...and...nothing. All sex took place indoors! Boring.

Is there a great rain sex scene in literature? I can't think of one although Fitzgerald did write a masterful rain flirtation scene when Daisy and Gatsby reunite at Nick's cottage. There are many great rain sex scenes in cinematic history and my clear favorite is Sigourney Weaver and Mel Gibson in *The Year of Living Dangerously*. I saw that film exactly one time, during my senior year in high school and have never forgotten their spontaneous embrace in rain. As for television and rain, all I can come up with is Detective Columbo and the rumpled raincoat he wore in Los Angeles while solving homicides. During the entire series, rain never fell. Still, I love the show.

RAIN: a love story

A NEW PATH

She called out of the gray around the time of the summer solstice. I had never expected to hear from her again after our estrangement, but I knew she knew that we had some sort of unfinished destiny together. In the past, social decorum had thwarted our obvious intense connection. We exuded a mystery achievement that unnerved others.

If I am honest with myself, I have to admit that she is the model for the woman I want to take on the world with and combat the insidious malaise of *whatever*. She knew rain too, its relentless, rugged magic because she had grown up in Kesey Country and had more ecstatic rain stories than anyone I'd ever met. But, through all our fascinating history, we didn't have a rain story together.

Long ago, I'd deleted her from my list of contacts so I didn't recognize the number when she phoned. I answered anyway; it was a weekday afternoon and Sonny and I relaxed on the deck with no particular place to go. And perhaps the call was from a saturnine literary agent imprisoned in an air conditioned cubicle in a far flung city who had read my one-sentence query about a fictionalized non-fiction book on rain and thought it was the greatest idea she'd ever heard of and would make a monumental addition to the scant literary canon on creative non-meteorology.

I couldn't believe it was her. No one seems to surprise me anymore, least of all people seeking contrition or an education in rain.

Within minutes she recounted a story of overwhelming psychic distress and that she had to come to the ocean, see me, and discuss the situation. I told her to visit as soon as possible. She told me she was driving down that weekend.

She brought rain, a huge late afternoon storm that vexes the tourist families expecting summer on the Oregon Coast in summer. It was the kind of June storm I absolutely love because if they didn't arrive with any regularity, there'd be millions of people vacationing here instead of the typical thousands sequestered indoors, complaining about rain on their gadgets instead of toying with it in the unscripted wild.

I stood under the awning and watched her car pull into the driveway. She was soaked by the time she walked to the deck. We embraced in rain and I felt the water in her hair, one of the most incredible sensations of my life. We said "sorry" to one another, and she handed me the quintessential rain beer in summer—Cerveza Pacifico. Our silent erosion was over.

We sat atop the spruce picnic table under the awning and stayed partially dry. I asked questions and we drank half the beer during her wrestling match with the answers. The storm picked up and the wind carried stacks of rain at a 45-degree angle down the street on an irregular conveyer belt. At some point, everything darkened around us, signaling the time to head outside, meet rain headlong, and advance the conversation into wetter realms. It was her idea and I didn't balk. Do you ever say "no" to rain? I did once and have regretted that decision ever since.

She grabbed the rest of the beer while I hustled up our coats. I brought along a film camera and we started walking through the neighborhood in search of adventure, which meant exploring the crumbling back yards of homes on the cliff overlooking the beach. Most homes were vacant the entire year, their absentee owners rained out of visiting or maintaining them.

It was practically a gale now and after some soggy reconnoitering, we settled on a narrow deck with a metal awning that initially looked like it might shelter us from the storm. The deck practically hanged over the beach. Inevitable erosion would euthanize this home in less than a decade and there was nothing the owners could do about it, not even prescribe riprap.

We found some decrepit wooden chairs and swept off the water. I noticed an uncovered barbecue disintegrating from rust. She lit a cigarette and it struggled to burn. I searched for a hidden key to the home; there might be ancient Canadian whiskey in some dank cabinet and I wanted whiskey.

The awning proved useless since rain blew upward and across instead of down. I took out the camera and shot away as she smoked, drank and laughed, knowing none of the photographs would turn out. I just wanted to try and focus through the condensation and capture the image of rain streaked across her face in a way that reminded me of an immortal line from the Beach Boys' "Good Vibrations," *I don't know where but she sends me there*. Interesting, the best sun band of all time sang my favorite line about a rainy woman's incalculable influence on me.

In rain, a path for her future emerged, and, with more rain, who knows where it will ultimately lead her.

As for myself, I continue to follow rain's path and like where it has led me so far.

DECEMBER 17, 2012

An old friend from my earliest days on the Oregon Coast, a classicist of rain, sat across from me in a Newport café. She's a wonderful writer of nature and one of the wisest people I know.

I drank black coffee and she ate green soup. We hadn't talked in a long, long time. Rain might have been falling or maybe not. I can't remember, nor is it important to remember. Lightless December is like that here.

At some point during our emotional conversation about a mutual friend, a deceased Jesuit priest named Andy Duffner, who is the only man I have ever met to achieve Nirvana, she somewhat slyly changed the subject.

"I heard you're writing a book about rain."

"That's right."

"I have to tell you, I used an umbrella in Portland when I walked to work and it was raining hard."

"What? No!"

"It was a four-mile walk to the library and I had to cross a bridge. I could see more around me when I used an umbrella. I could see people and they couldn't see me watching them."

"Please tell me it wasn't one of those big colorful golf contraptions favored by tanned Republicans."

"No, much smaller. It was like a little hermitage in there and no one could see me when I was watching them in the rain."

"Did you say hermitage?"

"Yes."

I snapped to literary attention and then slunk back in my chair. A trusted friend and connoisseur of rain had told me she sees more in rain when she uses an umbrella.

I thought I saw everything in the world without one.

Should I purchase an umbrella and conduct an experiment? Yes, I will, but I'll do it in Coos Bay where nobody knows me.

DECEMBER 19, 2012

Waves of rain broke over the bow of the bus as we approached an uprooted alder canopied across the undulating northbound lane of Highway 229. I saw the tree but Mike the bus driver did not. He was looking at me in his rearview mirror while happily delineating the merits of playing video games.

Mike turned around just in time to see his bus smack through a barricade of branches and produce a cacophony of colliding wood, metal and glass that coincided with a dip in the road that sent us flying a foot off the ground and then back to earth with a resounding thud. A chorus of teenage screams exploded from the back of the bus.

"Now that's rock and roll," said Meagan, one of my students seated behind me.

Mike never uttered a word nor pulled over. On the contrary, he sped up and I admired his zeal and pluck to transport my journalism class to the reservation of the Confederated Tribes of the Siletz as part of our investigation of local Native American issues for a forthcoming special edition of our magazine. I'd felt keen anticipation about this field trip for months because I knew I would have the opportunity to ask a Siletz Council member if his tribe had a rain song.

Some two hours later, my students and I sat entranced around a cedar fire in the Siletz Dance House and heard Bud Lane sing his enthralling song about a whale and Yaquina Head. He finished and asked if there were any questions.

"Do the Siletz people have a rain song?" I said.

Bud paused for a moment and the fire spit up a shower of sparks.

"No, we don't." He paused again.

"But we should." Another pause.

"I might have to create one."

DECEMBER 20, 2012

Christmas approaches and my senior English students in second period cling to their sanity by the flimsiest of fog. It has rained 3.39 inches since midnight with thankfully no end in sight. We might reach five inches today, a narcotic level when the going gets weird and the weird turn pro. I turned pro a long time ago and know exactly what to do: dragoon the rookies into my professionalism.

My culminating, transcendent lesson on *Siddhartha* is poised to awaken students to the awesome ecological and spiritual possibilities of eternally belonging to the water cycle. They generally prefer it to the Crucifixion and the Rapture. No gentle and merciful rain in those endings. Rain never judges by the way.

Unfortunately, this lesson will have to wait forever because rain invites us outside *right now* with crooked little fingers and a much better lesson. To refuse such an invitation constitutes a crime against making medicine to heal the world. It might also result in a violation of at least a dozen district safety policies.

What is this invitation, this better lesson? Buy my seniors a sustainable Christmas present and show them where the money goes.

I lead the seniors once more into the watery breach and we begin sprinting to the thrift store adjacent to campus. They have 10 minutes and four choices for gifts: book, record, cassette or VHS tape. I told them all proceeds from the store benefit the county animal shelter. We will save lives by buying junk.

You haven't lived until you've seen 30 high school seniors running to a thrift store in a deluge screaming "LITERATURE!" like the way Captain Picard said it in *Star Trek: The Next Generation.*

As students ransack the joint with their teen angst all aglow, I behold a wall of cassette tapes. Within seconds, I see Kenny G's *Breathless* and pull it out already knowing the inevitable. Side one, track three: "In the Rain." Price: 25 cents.

No. I can't do it. My journalism instincts fail me. I cannot bear the thought of listening to murder. I replace the cassette on the shelf and investigate the travel section of the books.

I already know what's there, untouched and molding for years. Thirty seconds later, I peruse *Oregon: Adventures in Time and Place*, published in 1987, the standard elementary grade textbook all Oregon public school fifth graders still use in their one and only required year of studying Oregon. In the book's narrative, Coos Bay thrives as timber town and wild salmon haven't yet disappeared because most Oregon teachers hadn't bothered to teach Oregon students that hatchery salmon are bogus and mask a century-old ecological crisis in Oregon's watersheds.

Digging for information on rain, I come across this arresting sentence: "Some places on the coast get more than 100 inches of rain a year. That is over 8 feet, which is as high as some classroom ceilings."

There it is. After much searching, I finally discovered the perfect simile to illustrate rain in my life, and... it appears in a children's book! Somehow, that makes perfect sense.

Oregon: Adventures in Time and Place does not mention Ken Kesey. Fifteen minutes later, students streak through rain back to class hoisting their gifts in the sky. Who would have ever thought that today's teenagers could get so excited about VHS tapes.

I spent $4.40 and gave the shelter a $50 tip. I like to believe I sent the spirit of Christmas rain happily into unknown corners.

DECEMBER 21, 2012

The last day of school before the holiday break was canceled today. A press release on the district's web site read:

> The Superintendent said a combination of reasons prompted him to make this decision: the potential for inclement weather conditions (sic) that make driving hazardous; the heightened level of concern, locally and nationally, about school security; and the high number of student absences that typically occur before a holiday or break.

In other words, officials canceled school because of the threat and dread of existential rain.

DECEMBER 22, 2012

On December 16, 1805, about a week before the Corps of Discovery moved into Fort Clatsop, their winter quarters on the Oregon Coast, William Clark wrote in his journal:

> Rained all the last night   we Covered our Selves as well as we Could with Elk Skins, & Set up the greater part of the night, all wet   I lay in the water verry Cold, the 5 men who Stayed out all night joined me this morning Cold & wet, The rain Contines, with Tremendious gusts of wind The winds violent   Trees falling in every derection, whorl winds, with gusts of rain Hail & Thunder, this kind of weather lasted all day, Certainly one of the worst days that ever was

William Clark was the most perfunctory rain complainer in American literary history. Interestingly enough, the word "rain" was one of the few words he never misspelled.

Meriwether Lewis, who suffered the surliest writer's block in American literary history during his stay at Fort Clatsop, also wrote perfunctorily on the subject of rain. Below is his daily weather report for December 1805:

1st	rained last night and Some this morning.

1st   rained last night and Some this morning.

2nd   rained all the last night and untill meridian
         cloudy the remainder of the day

3rd   rained all the last night & to day untill meridan and became fair
         & c.

4th   rained all day

5th   rained all last night and today
         I return to Capt Clark I mis him

6th   rained last night and all day to day
         wind not violent in the after part of the day
         fair in the eving.

7th   rained from 10 to 12 and at 2 P M.
         leave Pt. William

8th   Cloudy after a moderate rain last night.

9th   cloudy and rained moderately untill 3 P M.

10th   a violent wind last night 6 to 9 P M.
         river fast with rain. rained all day

11th   rained moderately all last night and to day

12th   rain

13th   Rain. need whisky

14th   rain

15th   rained all last night and untill 8 A. M to day after which it was
         Cloudy all day.

16th   rained all the last night.
         air Cold wind violent from the S W.
         accompanied with rain.—

17th   rained all last night and to day untill 9 A M when we had a
         Shower of hail for an hour and Cleared off.

18th   rained Snowed and hailed at intervales all the last night and to
         day untill meridian.

19th   rained (and hailed) last night and Several Showers of Hail and rain to day.   the air Cool.

20th   Some rain and hail last Night   the rain Contd. untill 10 a. m
21st   rained last night and to day
22nd   rain
23d   rained all last night and moderately to day with Several Show
         ers of Hail accompanied with hard Claps of Thunder and
         Sharp Lightning.
24th   rained at intervales last night and to day.
25th   rain. cant stop masturbatin
26th   raind with violent wind all last night and to day with Hard
         Claps of thunder & Sharp Lightning.
27th   rained moderately last night and to day
28th   rain
29th   rain untill 7 a.m. after
         Cloudy the remained of the day
         wind hard from the S E.
30th   Hard wind & rain last night.
         o day tolerably fair.
31st   rained last night and moderately all day to day.

What really happened to Meriwether Lewis during his winter on the
Oregon Coast? We know he later lost his mind and committed suicide.
I have a theory and sometimes fiction better illuminates theories rather
than journalism.

Rain is falling tonight as I write this from a moldy motel room in Astoria
not far from where Meriwether Lewis bivouacked. I've always wanted to
try my hand at a piece of historical fiction with Meriwether Lewis, surely
one of the most overrated figures in American history and a certified
weakling in Oregon rain, as the antagonist. So here goes, and I dedicate

this short story to all the sanctimonious members of the Lewis and Clark Priesthood who naively believe the famous journals contain the whole story, not understanding the obvious tenet that no one keeping a journal ever tells the whole story, or even bothers telling the truth all the time.

Like this journal of rain.

The Unofficial Journal

Meriwether Lewis slammed his quill pen into the desk; it splintered into a hundred shards that littered the floor of Fort Clatsop. Near the door, Seaman snored as wood smoke drifted into every crevice of the damp room.

He read the misspelled note again and shook his head. How could Clark do this to him?

Outside, rain fell for the hundredth day in a row. Inside, it fell too. The Corps of Discovery were away, hunting elk, fishing or bartering for sex.

Seaman farted. Lewis looked out the window and saw nothing but black and water. Rain on the coastal plain was driving the good captain insane. He couldn't write anything interesting in his journals; he couldn't sleep; he was out of booze; he was molding; he dreamed only in gray; he soon had to walk 2000 miles back to America, and worst of all, his boyfriend was in love—with a woman—no, a girl, an Indian girl!

Yes, William Clark had turned his tender affections toward Sacagawea. Lewis had seen it coming at Christmas, when she gave Clark the ermine scarf and he started openly calling her Janey, even in front of her husband, the craven Charbonneau, who didn't care because he was in love with the French fiddler Cruzette.

Clark's note made it clear: "I cannot luve you anymore. Can you ever imajin a time when we could be together out in the open? I mite as well fall in love with York! Or free him? There is something in the way she moves me and I must see this out. Plese forgive me. We'll always have the snow."

Lewis pounded the table with his fist. Clark was a fool! There was no way he could return to civilization and take up with an Indian woman! What an ingrate! Clark's mediocre career was going nowhere until this command and his phony co-captain rank! One letter to Jefferson from Lewis and Clark would find himself forever posted on the frontier with nothing to do but whip his misbehaving troops, York and occasionally himself.

Worst of all, Clark had recently whispered something to Lewis, in confidence, away from the malcontented men wracked with venereal disease and sobriety: "I am beginning to like rain."

Lewis stood up from the table. He went to the window and extended his hand into rain, caught a puddle, and rubbed it into his face. He hated rain. It seemed like every drop brought a little hammer down upon his brain and loins.

The journal rested on the table. The official journal that is, with all its clinical descriptions of flora and fauna and adventuring. The science stuff was true enough but the rest of the official journals was mostly fiction and Lewis loved the idea of a secret homosexual creating a virile and manly American myth for a new nation, dreaming of the day when the journals would be published and make him rich and famous. He might even make it on a unit of currency and he didn't even own a slave.

Another thicker journal rested on the table, the unofficial honest one he'd started at Fort Mandan when he first kissed Clark, and they took off all their clothes and made angel wings in the snow. Lewis had loved the snow and the cold at Mandan. It had exhilarated him. But rain and the wet in this new dank green country were something sinister he couldn't tolerate or hope to understand.

Lewis opened the unofficial one, found another quill, dipped it in ink, and began to write: "He'll get over her. I just have to be patint and perhaps bathe more…tell him how much I admirre his maps…if only rain would stop falling…"

DECEMBER 28, 2012

I couldn't believe what the mailwoman brought today: a glossy brochure from the Portland Art Dealers Association with a handwritten note affixed to the cover: "Saw this and thought of the project you're working on. Happy new rain year!"

Blackfish Gallery will host a show called "Rain" featuring "23 new views of precipitation." It opens January 3 in Portland, past the deadline to complete this book. There is no deadline for rain, by the way.

The press release states:

> Artist Members interpret the myriad aspects of rain in a group show of two and three-dimensional works. Topics explored include: weather forecasting; water scarcity; the aesthetics of clouds and sky; rain as a metaphor in poetry and literature; water as a natural resource; and more.

I have to see this show. The person who mailed me the brochure also wrote in the note, "It might inspire you and would be interesting to see what others are thinking of the same subject."

You know who mailed me the brochure? It was the same woman who broke up with me after I confiscated her umbrella and fed it to the sea lions in Yaquina Bay. I think she is finally on the verge of understanding rain, which would be the best thing in the world for her.

DECEMBER 29, 2012

No measurable precipitation yesterday. Nothing happening now. According to various reports, this is the second wettest year in Newport history and rain need only drop .05 more inches in the next 72 hours to reach 90 inches for 2012. I want 90. Give me 90 inches of juice or give me death! In 15 years of sheltering in the Rainlands, I have never attained this spectral level. I know something strange and wonderful will result if we come together at 90 inches.

The forecast, however, calls only for clouds. I must be the only person on the Oregon Coast who craves rain to fall immediately.

The poet Arthur Rimbaud once wrote in letter to a friend, "Advance always." I listen to poets.

Thus, if rain won't fall in Newport, I will advance into the places where it is raining and have my 90 inches. I will travel to the rainiest place in the state, located along the western slopes of the Oregon Coastal Range and go look at the hysterical crashing of rain merge into tributaries of swift-moving rivers in the Valley of the Giants, the ghost logging town of Valsetz and Mount Laurel.

It can rain 200 inches a year there.

Past Siletz, Nashville, Summit, higher, deeper, into the forested mountains exploding green gauze and gelatinous chlorophyll everywhere. I see a herd of elk steaming in a field, corroding Christmas lights, marijuana growing in the misty hollows, American and Confederate flags of red, white and blue and moldy green, downed limbs from Douglas firs, rusted Nashes, Ramblers and Tuckers, a black cat crouching in a glistening pasture, trailers streaked with mildew, animal fads such as miniature horses, dwarf goats, llamas and ostriches. I see human fads too, trampolines listing in six inches of water and overturned ATVs. Roads curve underneath sagging trestles, across dead train tracks, and I see television aerials and satellite dishes leaning in the trees, alders rooted from the roofs of ancient RVs, cows grazing in regenerating clearcuts, holly and apple orchards grown old, unpicked and wise, and a hidden mossy monument to the first school in Lincoln County (1866), where surely worked the rainiest teacher in Oregon history. Her name was Elizabeth Lee Porter.

I encounter a small child playing in the road with a radio-controlled car. I slow down and ask him about rain. He stares at me, says nothing. I drive on and encounter an old man in waders and rubbers carrying mail across the road. I slow down and ask him about rain. We make dull eye contact but he never slows his gait. He doesn't say a word and disappears into an unkempt laurel hedge larger than his house.

This is Richard Brautigan's *Short History of Oregon* redux.

An hour later, I find the rainiest place in Oregon, park in a puddle, get out of the truck, and start walking with my eyes closed into a clearing with my hands, palms up, raised to the sky.

The sun comes out.

I know what this means: *Sometimes a Great Notion* has just retained the title as the greatest book on rain in the history of Oregon literature.

DECEMBER 31, 2012

The sun is shining brightly today — time to conclude my exploration of walking in rain. Thank you for joining me. Did I get you to reconsider rain? I think that was my intention.

At the beginning of this book I said I would answer two monumental questions of rain posed by Creedence Clearwater Revival. *Have you ever seen the rain?* Yes, at long last. It took decades. *Who will stop it?* No one except me.

Ken Kesey wrote my second favorite all-time line about rain: "Comin' down like a cow wettin' on a flat rock. Like ten cows...like a goddam hundred." That, dear saturated reader, is the truest sound of hard, unrelenting rain on the Oregon Coast.

My third favorite line about rain comes from Richard Hugo: "The forces of righteousness, me and my friends, are praying for a storm, one of those grim dark rolling southwest downpours that will leave the electorate sane."

The politics of rain are sanity. Is it any wonder that the majority of the electorate from states of the sun-stained former Confederacy is totally insane? Or that the current Speaker of the US House of Representatives who wants to ruin the country with a fetishized ideology benefitting the rich has regular tanning appointments?

Shakespeare wrote my fourth favorite line about rain. In *Merchant of Venice*, Portia said:

> The quality of mercy is not strain'd,
> It droppeth as the gentle rain from heaven
> Upon the place beneath. It is twice blest:
> It blesseth him that gives and him that takes.

Rain is pure unadulterated mercy and people must teach mercy. I try to practice it every day of my life, especially when it comes to my students.

You have read my book about rain because I published it myself because no other publisher in the country would consider publishing it. "Too regional," they all said. "It won't sell 10,000 copies," they added. Rain is too regional but I will sell 20,000 copies of this book in Oregon alone. The fanatics in the Rainlands are out there, they find me every day. I hope this book alternately reads like scripture, survival guide, recreational brochure, sensual atlas and instructional manual to them.

During this eccentric exploration of Oregon's greatest leitmotif, I learned:

- The reasons for the demise of a special romantic relationship; rain enabled my understanding. Some might scoff at this belief, but going deep into the ravine of rain in a moment of intense emotional crisis saved me. This strategy might work for others as well. It certainly couldn't hurt anyone.
- Thinking about rain is a healthy existential pastime. Rain is alive and

enlivens you to possibilities in Oregon, many of them sensual.

- Walking on the beach in rain with Sonny is how I become a better person and teacher.
- I can blame only one thing on rain—this book.
- Raymond Carver wrote a short poem called "Rain" where the narrator wakes up on a rainy morning and decides to stay in bed and read all day and, "put myself entirely in the keep of this rainy morning." I love this poem because it taught me another way of advancing into rain without actually going outside.
- People love talking about rain.
- Rain is the greatest collaborator I have ever known.
- That after listening to hundreds of songs about rain, my favorite one is "Rain" by the Beatles, but not their version. My preferred rendi tion of "Rain" was performed by two of my students, Erica Redman and Andrew Johnson, at the weekly open mic session known as the Friday Lunch Jam that I host in my classroom. See and listen for your self at (http://www.youtube.com/watch?v=jUsY0yroN-s) By the way, it was raining like hell during their performance.
- That the most bizarre thing about rain I encountered in the writing of this book was a South Korean pop band called Vodka Rain. Please Google them, watch their videos, and report back to me. I want to understand.
- I might foment a ballot initiative to ban the sale of umbrellas in Or egon. It would pass in a rainslide.
- That the sexiest thing I heard about rain during the writing of this book was from a woman who said she liked having sex in the bed of her pickup truck when it rained so she could hear the sound of rain striking the canopy. Apparently, it made her wild.
- Walking in rain makes me long for a return stint as a sportswriter cov ering high school football for a Tillamook newspaper. I recently reread those articles; my passion to write about rain clearly began

there and I never saw a single umbrella on the sidelines.

• I do not want to become a Stamper from *Sometimes a Great Notion* and end up recalcitrant by rain. I do not want to adopt their family's "Never give a inch," black and white, intransigent mentality in a place of perpetual gray.

• That my intense contemplation of rain completely washed away the partitions between fact and fiction in my writing; rain has suggested a new direction for my future literary and teaching endeavors.

• That quite possibly, I wrote this book on rain because I teach at New port High School, the greatest accidental rain high school in the country because it was designed by a Southern Californian architect whose ludicrous blueprint called for a flat (and therefore leaky) roof, and the preposterous routine of making students walk in rain across campus to change classrooms. Newport High School students are the most accomplished runners in rain in the annals of American public education. Some of the teachers excel too. I have never seen an umbrella in use on campus in my five years of teaching at Newport High School.

• That the best indoor place to watch rain on the Oregon Coast is sit ting at the back table of the Triangle Tavern in Astoria. The second best is the Port Dock One Bar in Newport.

• That the saddest thing about rain on the Oregon Coast is watching the dairy cows standing in it for long hours without shelter. They certainly don't have a romance with it.

• That rain on the Oregon Coast is stone rain. According to the Oxford English Dictionary, the adjective "stone" is defined as, "occasionally as a mere intensive (= very completely)" as in stone asleep, stone cold, stone deaf, stone dumb, stone hard and stone naked. Think "Stone Free" by Jimi Hendrix, "Stone Love" by the Supremes, and "I Am Stone in Love With You" by the Stylistics. Yes, stone rain it is. Everybody start using that phrase and give me credit.

- The word "rain" used as a noun should never be preceded by the article "the." Rain is big enough to stand alone.

The best and final thing I learned about rain was discovering its ultimate crucible. Let me illustrate: I just came back from walking the neighbor's dog in the Sunday afternoon rain. I saw an elderly neighbor kneeling at the edge of his lawn. He wore gray sweats without corporate university logos and black rubber boots covered in mud. No cap. I went over to him.

"Doing yard work in rain?" I said.

"It makes me feel like a kid, you know, playing, getting dirty?"

I knew something about that.

"You know, the NFL playoff games are on right now," I said.

"What's the NFL?"
I think he was joking. Two seconds later he said, "I play in the ORL."

"What's that?"

"The Oregon Rain League."

He had mastered the test long ago and was obviously enlightened in a rain-Nirvana-sort-of-way.

The crucible of rain is deciding to advance into it or not. To advance into rain is to love it, or at least accept what it has to offer and not let it deter or defer.

I want to close my book on rain with another immortal line from *Sometimes a Great Notion*: "It has commenced. He hears the rain on the roof, like soft nails being driven into the rotten wood. It has commenced all right. And it will go on for six months." I hear that same soft Kesey sound as I tap away on the Italian typewriter in concert with rain. Do you realize I finished this book at precisely the same time rain will go on for six more months? Another big story of rain is about to begin, but this one is done.

In 2012, according to the weather station at the Hatfield Marine Science Center, it rained 89.97 inches in Newport.

POSTscript

Rain lashed the landscape as a midnight in January approached. I was staying in a coastal Oregon town where they say it rains a hundred inches a year, working on my book about rain.

The phone rang and I took the call.

She said, "You better be real about this rain stuff because I'm walking to your place and I'm going to be soaked."

It sounded like the best threat I'd ever heard in my life.

I told her: "I got into the tequila"

"That's good. I got into the pot."

I had met someone who worshipped *Sometimes a Great Notion* and she was walking stoned in stone rain to see me. I couldn't wait to see her.

An hour later, I heard a knock on the door. I barely had the knob turned before she pushed through the jamb not unlike what I imagine Samson did with the pillars. He brought down the house if you recall.

She was completely nude and covered in rain.

I let her in. I tasted her rain.

ACKNOWLEDGEMENTS

AND MISCELLANY

First and foremost, I give thanks to rain. It invited, beguiled and wrung this book out of me.

Amira Shagaga conceived and executed the design of the book. She has become my most valued creative collaborator and one of my special friends. Frank Boyden's incredible etchings of rain sharpened the aesthetic of this book in a way that I didn't envision until he toured me through his studio on Cascade Head and proceeded to blow my mind. Thank you Frank. Anyone interested in purchasing the etchings included in this book should contact the Laura Russo Gallery in Portland. In recent years, Sarah Kolesar has been my best editor and she proved that again with this book. Tiffany Gordon provided timely transcriptions of documents. Domenica Gavin and Brie Staunton turned in hard-nosed proofreading jobs. In record time, Emily Ferguson whipped up a savage mix of blues songs about rain that helped me finish the book. She also gave me shrewd comments on the manuscript. Audrey Guerena's friendship and enthusiasm for my literary mission are two of the great joys of my life. Elise Ulmer put me onto a few new things about rain. Sorry about the umbrella. Gerry Lewin took the Tom McCall photograph and allowed me to include it. Much obliged Gerry. I hope I have never disappointed with my use of your indelible Oregon historical images. Werner Herzog's *Of Walking in Ice* was a major inspiration for this book. I urge readers to seek out and find this odd and wonderful little tome.

My web page designer Lena Burdett has proved indispensible in my success as an independent publisher. Tim Sproul and Angie Collins were instrumental in helping me occasionally *cut through* and relax. Chanah Sheldon guided me through some tough times prior to writing this book and I am eternally grateful. Dave and the crew at Pioneer Printing once again performed their excellent service for Nestucca Spit Press. I love keeping it local. I have incredibly supportive parents and that condition always contributes to an author's ideas coming to fruition. Ken Kesey's writing continues to imbue me. I wish I could have met him. Oregon's publicly-owned beaches had a lot to do with this book. I owe practically all my writing and spiritual life to the immortal Oregon gods who preserved the ocean beaches for me to use and never have to pay a cent for the privilege. Your big epic book is next. *Hipfish* magazine and its editor Dinah Urell deserve recognition for running my "On Rain" column for a year. Many of these pieces became part of the book. Jamie Ehrke was an outstanding reader of early drafts. I want to single out my principal, Jon Zagel. He's backed me unconditionally more times than I can remember. I present unique challenges to any principal and Jon's unwavering trust in me is much appreciated. Thank you, Legion of the Rock. One of these days, other mortals will experience the sublime and holy influence of your awesome power and decode the map of the delta that leads to the undiscovered country. I am sure it rains a lot there.

Readers may be interested to know that I came up with many alternate titles for this book before deciding on *Of Walking in Rain.* They were: *Down with Rain, The Crucible of Rain, The Rainlands, On Rain, Rain On Rain: A Love Story, Stone Rain, Oregon Rain, Gimme Rain, Call Me Rain, No Retreat from Rain, Rainy Day Man #1, Season of Rain, The Raining, Box of Rain, Opened, Hard Rain Fell, The Language of Rain, The Reign of Rain, Rain Me, Rain You, Born to Rain, Rain it Slant, Rain Never Sleeps, The Ruth of Rain, The Erudition of Rain, Tangled Up in Rain.*

I owe substantial gratitude to all my students at Newport High School. They gushed forth a fountain of inspiration and wrote well on rain, took incredible photographs of rain and indulged my obsession with rain. They are the greatest rain students in the annals of American public education.

Poetry really isn't my forte but every now and then I feel inspired to write a poem. A couple months into 2013, a big rainstorm elicited this:

Double Shot of Rain

I don't get it.
Why don't we just run naked
in rain
and dive into the ocean?

If we could all go under
in rain,
we'd all get it.
World peace at last.
Make rain, not war.

You'll do it,
go under,
in rain,
with me.

I can see you,
through the keyhole of the limpet,
those hips,
turned west,
both of us drunk on wine
we've brought to the sea.

We'd hold the bottle to the sky,
let rain find a way in,
like rain does,
if you allow,
or beckon.

I would push you down,
splash wine onto your stomach.
It would pool with rain
in the universe of your navel.
Then I would drink the potion.

You probably wouldn't say a word,
which is everything there is worth saying.

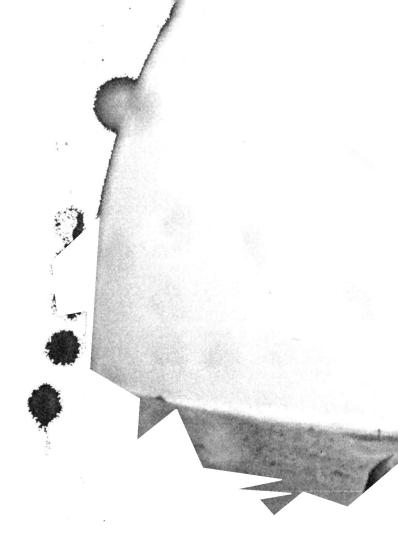

And my final thanks goes to...
Sonny the husky.

What will I do without you?
Rain will never be the same.

Matt Love grew up in Oregon City and is the publisher
of Nestucca Spit Press and author/editor of *The Beaver State Trilogy,*
Citadel of the Spirit: Oregon's Sesquicentennial Anthology,
The Newport Trilogy and *Gimme Refuge: The Education of a Caretaker.*

In 2009, Love won the Oregon Literary Arts' Stewart H. Holbrook Literary
Legacy Award for his contributions to Oregon history and literature.
He lives in South Beach and teaches at Newport High School.
You can reach him at lovematt100@yahoo.com.
He'd love to hear your rain story.